D0940716

THE THESIS AND THE BOO.
A GUIDE FOR FIRST-TIME ACADEMIC AUTHORS

Edited by Eleanor Harman, Ian Montagnes, Siobhan McMenemy, and Chris Bucci

The academic caveat 'publish or perish' is not new, and for over a quarter of a century *The Thesis and the Book* has come to the aid of graduate students in their quest for publication. The doctoral dissertation, usually the first book-length study completed by a scholar, is only rarely publishable as a book. Understanding the differences between the two forms is a crucial part of one's education as a scholar and is equally important in appreciating the endeavours of scholarly publishers. *The Thesis and the Book: A Guide for First-Time Academic Authors*, revised and expanded in this second edition, continues to provide the best overview of the process of revising a dissertation for publication.

Drawing on the expertise of the contributors, all of whom are editors, publishers, and scholars themselves, the chapters present the essential differences between a thesis and a book (including matters of purpose and audience), give guidance on the necessary stylistic, technical, and structural revisions to the dissertation, and offer advice to first-time authors who must not only revise their work to satisfy prospective publishers, but also become familiar with the workings of scholarly publishing.

The Thesis and the Book will continue to be of great value to graduating doctoral students seeking publication and to the faculty members who supervise these students. It will also be of value to acquisitions editors at scholarly presses, who must contend with the submission of revised dissertations for publication.

ELEANOR HARMAN was founding editor of *Scholarly Publishing: A Journal for Authors and Publishers*.

IAN MONTAGNES was formerly editor-in-chief of University of Toronto Press. He is currently a publishing consultant.

SIOBHAN McMENEMY is an acquisitions editor at University of Toronto Press and an instructor in the publishing program at Ryerson University.

CHRIS BUCCI was formerly an acquisitions editor at University of Toronto Press. He is now an editor at HarperCollins Canada.

THE THESIS AND THE BOOK

A Guide for
First-Time Academic Authors

SECOND EDITION

Edited by

Eleanor Harman

Ian Montagnes

Siobhan McMenemy

Chris Bucci

UNIVERSITY OF TORONTO PRESS

Toronto Buffalo London

© University of Toronto Press Incorporated 2003
'An Academic Author's Checklist' © Barbara B. Reitt 2003
Toronto Buffalo London
Printed in Canada

ISBN 0-8020-8806-6 (cloth)
ISBN 0-8020-8588-1 (paper)

Printed on acid-free paper

National Library of Canada Cataloguing in Publication

The thesis and the book : a guide for fist-time academic authors /
Eleanor Harman ... [et al.]. – 2nd ed.

Includes bibliographical references and index.
ISBN 0-8020-8806-6 (bound)   ISBN 0-8020-8588-1 (pbk.)

1. Scholarly publishing.   2. Dissertations, Academic.   I. Harman,
Eleanor, 1909–1988

Z286.S37T54 2003   808'.02   C2002-905845-7

University of Toronto Press acknowledges the financial assistance to
its publishing program of the Canada Council for the Arts and the
Ontario Arts Council.

University of Toronto Press acknowledges the financial support for
its publishing activities of the Government of Canada through the
Book Publishing Industry Development Program (BPIDP).

Contents

Preface to the Second Edition

The Thesis and the Book, which was originally published in 1976 as a collection of articles culled from the venerable *Scholarly Publishing* (now the *Journal of Scholarly Publishing*), has become a classic among doctoral students and their supervisors. As Eleanor Harman and Ian Montagnes knew from their years of experience as scholarly press editors, first-time authors welcome guidance from the professionals as they begin the important revisions to the thesis and transform it into a publishable book manuscript. The aim of the manuscript, its intended audience, the language, style, and organization of the work: these are the kinds of concerns addressed by the contributors to this guide, who are themselves editors, publishers, and scholars. The success of the book attests to the soundness of their advice and the ongoing need of it.

More than ever before, scholars must heed the warning of the 'publish or perish' mantra that is intoned across the campus. For doctoral students, the obvious place to turn for the material for their first book is to their dissertations. It isn't surprising that the advice an editor might offer an author hasn't changed a great deal over the years, at least with respect to the stylistic and structural changes necessary when transforming a thesis into a book manuscript. Competition for the attention of acquisitions editors at university presses is fierce, however, given the prolif-

eration of graduate programs and the rising number of graduating doctoral students. As a result, the contributions to this second edition have been revised and expanded to reflect the needs
of the twenty-first-century scholar.

   With college and university curricula now reflecting a desire
among students for new forms of professional development –
courses on pedagogy, access to writing labs, and certificates in
editing and publishing – there is an expectation that scholars
new to the world of university presses will take it upon themselves to become familiar with the ins and outs of academic
publishing. It has become a crucial part of a graduate student's
education to learn as much as possible about prospective publishers and their publishing programs. Answers can be found
here to such questions as the following: How does one find the
right publisher for a given book project? What kind of material
is required in a formal proposal to a university press? How long
does it take for a scholarly book to appear in print? What is it,
exactly, that the publisher does for its authors? And how much
attention can an author expect to receive from the publisher
once the book has been published? Because the submission of a
carefully revised manuscript is not the *only* way to impress an
acquisitions editor, we present *The Thesis and the Book: A Guide
for First-Time Academic Authors* as the place to begin the quest for
publication of one's first scholarly book.

SIOBHAN McMENEMY

CHRIS BUCCI

Preface to the First Edition

The thesis or dissertation, prepared as part of a program of graduate study, is only rarely publishable as a book, and even more rarely as a good one. On the other hand, many books, and some good ones, have had their origins in dissertations or have been developed from research undertaken for a doctorate. The distinction between a thesis and a book is not, alas, always clear, either to the author of the thesis, anxious to secure early publication for the fruits of intensive study and laborious writing, or to some of his advisers, who may encourage the new graduate to submit his manuscript immediately for publication. The confusion arises in large part from a conflict between the traditional view that a dissertation should be publishable, and the practical imperative to produce a thesis which will convince a small committee of its writer's grasp of a restricted field of knowledge. The traditional approach to dissertations in graduate studies is criticized and defended by contributors to this volume. Nevertheless, despite all the lamentations about 'publish or perish,' publication continues to be essential for the professional advancement of most scholars, and particularly in attaining those first few vital rungs on the academic ladder.

While the author of a thesis may excusably be concerned with immediate benefits, neither he nor scholarly publishers can forget that publication has wider objectives, which include the author's own intellectual development through the criticism of his work by a broad readership of his peers. Even more important is the contribution that his ideas may make to the development of the discipline to which he belongs. What is not published, in one form or another, may be lost; and what is published, by the same token, should be in a form and style that make it easily available to all who can use it.

The dissertation can be preserved, and reach a minimal audience, by deposit in a university library or through such valuable programs as that operated for many years now by Xerox University Microfilms. Modern technology is rapidly providing other means of preserving and disseminating the results of research. The book, however, still remains the most effective method of all for easy reference anywhere, and the contributors to this work, in their remarks, mainly imply publication in the form of conventionally manufactured volumes. Nevertheless, the advice they offer can be applied with profit whatever form of reproduction is eventually used. All their suggestions lead to one end: to make the text more eloquent, more effective, and more easily accessible to the ultimate reader.

The contributions deal with differences in the form of presentation between the average dissertation and a publishable book. The viewpoints expressed range from broad questions of purpose and style, and of scholarly editing and publishing in general, to detailed practical suggestions for rewriting. All the chapters have previously appeared as articles in *Scholarly Publishing: A Journal for Authors and Publishers,* which is published by University of Toronto Press with generous support from the Canada Council. They are gathered here in the hope that they may benefit graduate students still writing their dissertations, those who have recently earned doctorates and now are seeking publication, faculty members supervising graduate students, and all others interested in good scholarly writing.

ELEANOR HARMAN

IAN MONTAGNES

Contributors

Francess G. Halpenny is the former managing editor of University of Toronto Press and is Professor Emeritus in the Faculty of Information Studies at the University of Toronto.

The late **Robert Plant Armstrong**, professor of anthropology at the University of Texas at Dallas, was a former director of Northwestern University Press.

William C. Dowling is a professor of English at Rutgers University and has written several articles for the *Journal of Scholarly Publishing* over the years.

Olive Holmes is the former editor of the East Asian Research Center (now the Fairbank Center for East Asian Research) at Harvard University and is an editor and indexer in Nobleboro, Maine.

Barbara B. Reitt is the principal of Reitt Editing Services in Highlands, North Carolina, and a co-founder and past president of the Board of Editors in the Life Sciences, which administers certification examinations for professional editors.

Allan H. Pasco is Hall Professor of Nineteenth-Century Literature at the University of Kansas and was a founder and, for several years, the general editor of the Purdue University Monographs in Romance Languages series.

THE THESIS AND THE BOOK:
A GUIDE FOR FIRST-TIME ACADEMIC AUTHORS

chapter one

The Thesis and the Book

FRANCESS G. HALPENNY

A press engaged in the publication of scholarly works is often asked whether it has a policy regarding the publication of theses. Its answer usually is that theses as such do not normally have a place in its publication program. They may do so only when they become suitable books. The following brief analysis of the difference between thesis and book will, it is hoped, be helpful to those who are contemplating further activity with the subject of their thesis once it has been approved, and might plan at some stage submission of a manuscript for book publication.[1] It does not begin to cover all the situations that can be encountered but does try to set forth some general principles. Other essays in this collection address methods of accomplishing the transition from thesis to book.

To some, making a distinction between a thesis and a book may seem to be only quibbling. After all, most theses in the humanities and social sciences (and it is to these fields that the following discussion is relevant) have the same general arrangement as books: they have a table of contents, a preface or introduction, a text divided into chapters, appendixes perhaps, illustrations often, and always a bibliography. The parallel similarity of outward form may be granted, but there is nevertheless a fundamental difference in the purpose for which all these separate parts are assembled in the case of a book and of a thesis, and there is often a fundamental difference in the techniques of presentation suitable to each.

A thesis presents a report of the investigation of its author into a carefully marked out segment of a topic or problem in literature or history or political science or economics or sociology. It is expected to marshal all the relevant information that the candidate has discovered in investigating this topic or problem, and so is a test of ability to gather evidence and arrange it. Each statement made must be documented so that the examiners may see how the author has built up the case being presented and may judge how sound it is. The candidate is really demonstrating his or her ability to carry on research. The audience to whom the demonstration is addressed is, of course, primarily the members of the examining committee. In addressing them, the candidate is normally expected to use a formal structure that has become the traditional format of theses.

It is only natural that, when the thesis has been approved, the author should give some attention to the possibility of its appearing in whole or in part on the printed page. Availability of its findings in the original thesis form need no longer be a concern, of course, now that microfilm, interlibrary loan, and electronic transfer can assume responsibility for distribution of the thesis document. Print is a different matter, however, and a decision about how to seek it, or whether to seek it at all, requires careful thought. A gap in time of at least a few months between approval of the thesis and re-examination of it with book publication in mind is usually wise so that the author may achieve some distance from it and therefore greater objectivity. The passage of time is well known to be beneficial in helping authors become effective editors of their own work.

When the writer makes this re-examination of the thesis, he or she may decide that the scope or nature of its theme does not admit of the expansion proper for a book subject or, and this is important, that he or she is no longer vitally interested in the theme and in undertaking any expansion that might be possible. An author who comes to either of these conclusions should cheerfully decide to let the thesis rest, recognizing that it has had an honourable life and performed its task in relation to the author's career, and that those who wish to consult it can do so with no great effort. It may, of course, be a source for a public lecture or a paper at a scholarly conference, or an article or two for periodicals. Good articles are always welcome and can serve perfectly well to bring the author's special contribution in the thesis to the attention of others in its particular field.

The author may, however, conclude that the thesis has been an opportunity to examine only part of a topic that challenges investigation and discussion and that might well be considered further with the broader and different requirements of book publication in mind. This conclusion should sensibly be accompanied by a realization that the scope and presentation suitable for a book will likely mean a good deal more work, and a determination to undertake it in the interests of the subject and the author's own reputation as a scholarly writer. It is also possible for an author to conclude, although confirmation from the examiners would be advisable before finally making up his or her mind, that the thesis presents a subject in a depth and organization that would seem already suitable for a book and requires not much more than the removal of the thesis format.

The description just given will perhaps suggest the background against which most scholarly presses have developed their procedures in relation to theses. Experience, and the pressure of growing numbers of doctoral candidates, have had an important influence. It will be appreciated that it is not feasible to invite submission of all theses offered as such, when it is certain that only a small percentage of them will be close to book manuscripts at this stage and all will have to undergo revision in varying degrees. Nor would it always be in the best interests of the authors themselves for full-scale consideration of most theses to be undertaken. Readers' reports on some theses have recommended that they be converted to articles but not to books; on others they have often called for revision on such a scale as to be tantamount to the production of a new work. The obtaining of these reports inevitably used up months the author could profitably have spent in rewriting and revision before submission. After revision, the book manuscript had, of course, to go through the whole process of consideration again. Pressure on the time and concentration of press editors who consider manuscripts has also to be remembered in this connection, as well as the expense and time involved in the securing of the reports of editorial readers and outside consultants.

Most presses, however, would not wish to discourage sensible enquiries. What can be suggested here to authors of theses is that they will normally be able to arrive themselves, after a judicious waiting period, and perhaps in consultation with their examiners, at the decision whether or not further work with their thesis should be contemplated. If the decision is that the thesis warrants revision toward a book manuscript, and the author can contemplate this revision with some enthusiasm, then he or she might well sound out possible publishing interest. A good way for an author to proceed is a carefully prepared letter, which outlines the history of the thesis (and indicates the examiners who know it), provides a curriculum vitae of the author, describes the content of the new manuscript that will be prepared (preferably with a table of contents), and gives a statement about the contribution to its scholarly field which it can be expected to make. This prospectus would be considered by a press editor (perhaps in consultation with an outside adviser), who would then report to the author whether the publishing house has an interest in principle in the proposed manuscript and whether it sees any value in looking at the thesis at this stage. Authors whose theses would seem to be ready for consideration as book manuscripts with not much more than technical changes might well receive an invitation to submit their work for preliminary examination in answer to their enquiry, although some independent assurance from an examiner might be sought first. A manuscript for which the author plans a major revision, and which interests the editor, will usually be followed up by the press at the time the author has said he or she expects to complete the revision. Formal consideration, and a decision about publication, takes place when a final manuscript is received.

The nature of the revision so often referred to above requires some discussion at this point. There are two principal considerations to be heeded in the development of a book manuscript from a thesis. The first is the new and larger audience to be addressed, and the second is the treatment of the material in a way that will best meet the needs and interests of this audience.

The new readers of a scholarly work may be imagined as a thousand or as five thousand in number. In general, however, whatever their number, the new readers will influence a revision in much the same way. The wider audience will, of course, include not just fellow workers in the subject, narrowly defined; many academic readers with many different interests will come to the book, not because of a special interest in the writer's main subject, but because what they happen to be working on or reading about touches this subject at a number of points. These readers, and sometimes others with even more general interests, will have to be persuaded to do more than pick up the book and glance at the index; the author has to think in terms of attracting their attention as he or she did not have to do with the small examining committee.

This challenge means that the author must at an early stage answer the question how much background information can be assumed in the book's audience. The answer will determine fundamentally how the author must present the material being offered. Two mistakes are possible: under-explanation (and under-documentation) or over-explanation (and over-documentation). It is never easy to find the safe and sensible course between the two; yet unless the need to attempt it is recognized, the conversion from thesis to book will be half-hearted and the result will lack force.

It is almost always true that a book prepared from a thesis requires an 'opening out' of the topic beyond the often narrow limits appropriate to a thesis. A writer for a wider public must give the manuscript's topic a context. He may extend the time span of the historical movement he is covering; she may include more writers or more influences in her effort of literary criticism; or, if they are warranted in giving attention primarily to the original subject, may support and illuminate it with a description of background that will add necessary perspective. In all this, the author will aim at a manuscript that is more or less self-contained, one that does not depend on a reader's having full familiarity with an array of people, places, and events before starting to read. The book manuscript should also lead up to the drawing of conclusions and inferences and should make judgments as it proceeds. Readers should feel that they have had the pleasure of listening to an informed person discussing a topic or a period and ordering it for their better understanding. This reaction at once suggests another most important difference between thesis and book: the difference in tone.

A thesis tends to be a formal document which has a rigid structure and is often written in 'academic' prose. Its author is not under the necessity of establishing direct communication with the reader, although by no means forbidden to do so. A book must provide a sense that the author is speaking directly to its audience. This in turn involves a commitment of the author to the book's subject. From its opening pages a scholarly work of analysis or criticism should impart to the reader the writer's conviction that the subject is worth writing about and worth reading about. The reader should want to go on. Successful persuasion will be found, among other things, to have a great deal to do with the manner in which the theme of the book is introduced. The introductory part of a book must not only lead logically to the heart of the study but lead readers to it, and engage them in it.

Style is another element that can do much to increase the sense of readers that they are in direct communication with the author. The indirect and carefully impersonal style often considered appropriate in a thesis can give a chill to the pages of a book. Simplicity and directness should be the aim. Jargon should be examined sceptically. An author should prefer for sentences the active and the alive to the passive and the unduly careful. He or she should endeavour to introduce light and air into the prose, by varying the length and structure of sentences, by making less use of 'It is important to note ...,' and 'It can be concluded that ...,' by omitting formal summaries or else working them in more skilfully and informally, by cutting down subheadings to the minimum in favour of smoother transitions in the text.

Revisions in the interest of engaging the attention of a wider audience, which may mean a sketching in of background or a wider context for the topic, and which will allow a more direct address and more open style of writing, can profitably be considered also for a lecture or an article prepared from thesis material. With either one, a different audience spoken to with a different purpose creates a need for a different approach to content and presentation. A chapter taken from a thesis with only a little adjustment will rarely delight listeners at a lecture or hold the attention of journal readers, however sound and original its argument may be.

Finally, a word about reference notes. These are omnipresent in theses, because they are largely the guarantees of the accomplishment of proper research. A great deal of this proof can be assumed for the purposes of a book – we do not need note references to well-known reference works for standard items of information about Canada or another country, or dates and a brief biography for, say, Voltaire when he first appears in a work of literary criticism. We do need references for quotations or for opinions with which disagreement is possible or for statements of fact presented for the first time or in a new light. All discussion of a point raised in the text should be given in the text unless there is justification for including in a note a remark that is genuinely – and briefly – parenthetical. A sequence of quotations from the same source running through a paragraph of text need have only one inclusive reference. The date of a newspaper editorial or of a debate in a legislature or the line numbers of a selection of poetry can be worked into the text and the note dropped. If there is to be a bibliography, it can be responsible for all the bibliographical details of works cited, and the notes can therefore be briefer and still useful.

In making the change from a thesis to a book manuscript, there may be a great deal to do or there may be comparatively little. Nevertheless each thesis must be rigorously subjected to the questions about audience and style set forth above. In finding the right way to address the contemplated audience, authors may well discover that the farther they leave the thesis behind, mentally and physically, the better the book they will write and the more people they will persuade to read it. A thesis should, in short, be a quarry from which a new structure is built.

NOTE

1 An article bearing the present title first appeared in *Press Notes* from the University of Toronto Press, May 1962, and a second version was printed in *Press Notes*, January 1968. The author would like to acknowledge the help of the late Professor F.E.L. Priestley, who collaborated in the first version.

chapter two

The Dissertation's Deadly Sins

ROBERT PLANT ARMSTRONG

The dissertation system must have laid at its door an enormous squandering of creativity, youth, time, and money each year upon the execution of prose works that do not communicate significantly and are therefore dysfunctional. The publisher, upon whom depends much of the scholar's success, usually refuses even to look at them. The system, the dissertation directors operating within it, and the writers contingent upon both all conspire to commit six grievous assaults upon discourse – sins, indeed, which alienate the writers and their work from that state of intellectual grace whose outward sign is serious, straightforward, responsible, and skilful communication. These assaults are amateurism, redundancy, trivialization, specializationalism, reductionism, and arrogance. One or all of these defects can usually be found in any given dissertation.

AMATEURISM

By regarding the dissertation as a pre-professional piece of work, the graduate school postpones its students' maturation and encourages in them contentment with amateurishness and unprofessionalism. Under the existing system, writers of dissertations have only limited opportunity to develop any real sense of their role in their respective fields of study. In what is in all probability the major intellectual enterprise thus far in their lives as scholars, they are accordingly held back by a sense of their own lack of worth. Within all but the hardiest this intolerable ambiguity results in debilitation of energy, enthusiasm, and resolve – buttressed by a biting and visceral sense of frustration. Both intellectually and emotionally, doctoral candidates are unprepared to undertake the task of writing for which they have no option. Professionally they are without locus, and personally, without a sense of fixity. Small wonder then that their control over whatever form they choose may be less than sure. And if their prose is unexciting, they are at least playing safe. If their work is part this and part that – part pre-professional and part professional – it reflects what they themselves are at the time of writing.

A second characteristic of the system makes the situation of doctoral candidates even more hopeless, insuring the lack of confidence and competence that produces amateurishness. For writers of dissertations are expected to undertake a caricature of learned discourse whose sententiousness intimidates them (perhaps it revolts them as well) and whose artificiality of form and rhetoric arouses hostility in anyone who has read real books and responded to that naturalness of structure in prose which is characteristic of the world beyond the seminar room.

Artificiality of form was perhaps more noticeable in the dissertation a decade ago than it is now, although one still encounters dissertations built upon the older model of 'statement of the problem, review of the literature, body of the dissertation, and a conclusion which must be more than a simple summary of what has preceded it.' At the very least this prescription creates a tiresome sameness in dissertations; at the worst it destroys the subtle plasticity that is required to set forth ideas effectively.

Artificiality of form is found today chiefly in the lingering propensity of dissertation directors to demand the inclusion of irrelevant demonstrations. Such demands inhibit the first-rate student's drive toward the clean, simple, direct discourse that leads immediately and resolutely to the point, along the path of least conceptual and formal resistance. The new writer, under the worst of directors, is carefully taught discursive obfuscation and dishonesty; under some others he or she perhaps learns only a slight dissembling; and under the best, no dishonesty at all. But too often straightforward thinking is stultified by methodological, conceptual, and informational prolixity.

Artificiality stems also from the dissertation's unspoken rules of rhetoric. That so few bad principles can generate such vast volumes of bad prose is hardly to be believed. The first of these principles is the cowardly conditional, by which dissertation writers remove themselves from the need to state a forthright fact in a forthright mood. I suspect that the dissertation uses more conditional sentences than does any other prose form in the language. The worst offenders in this respect are the social scientists. In these disciplines young scholars appear to learn early in their careers an inviolable relationship between truth and tortuous conditionality. Thus: *all things else being equal, it would appear to be the case that, under given circumstances, it may not be uncommon for writers of dissertations to execute certain prose styles which those who seem to like their English straight and strong might conceivably call a perversion of the language.*

The pusillanimous passive is a second characteristic of dissertational rhetoric. Its popularity is rooted in a notion that assertions in the passive voice are not only less forthright, but somehow also more objective than those with an active verb. But over-use of the passive robs prose of its vitality, and reduces it to a mishmash of inconclusiveness. The assumption that the passive voice lends objectivity is clearly nonsensical: *it is to be hoped that the use of the passive voice which is resorted to by writers of dissertations, to whose mastery of it is attributable reams of pages offensive to the educated ear, will be somewhat more markedly attenuated.* As this example indicates, outlandish diction makes its own contribution to the amateurishness of dissertation prose. When these three faults are forged into a common fabric, the effect is frightening.

The dissertation's amateurishness further reveals itself in pedantry and cowardice. The former is most notably manifested

in servility to that convention which forbids authors to say anything on their own, plaguing their readers instead with a note to
nearly every fact and opinion. I am confident that someone, in
referring to the earth's roundness, must have documented the
assertion with a reference to Esdras and Columbus.[1] The basis
of this slavery to notes is the same insecurity that produces the
cowardly involutions of style. Nor need it stop there. From
playing safe with facts and prose, the student passes to playing
safe with concepts, and thus loses probity.

REDUNDANCY

The six defects of the dissertation are not neatly separable. They
are closely related and interdependent. In defining redundancy
as that condition of discourse in which there is more prose than
information, we must not therefore be surprised to find several
of the qualities already discussed under amateurism.

Redundancy is of two kinds, structural-functional and informational. The first appears in such structural elements of the
dissertation as the review of the literature, which add little to
our understanding of the author's thesis. If we conceive of
structure itself as important in the progressive advancement of
the thesis, then anything that fails to contribute to that forward
movement, such as the review of literature, is anti-structural.
Then there are other elements of structural redundancy –
reviews of arguments that require no reviewing, extended
excursions into methodology first because this is expected and
then as an exercise for its own sake, excessive use of notes
which are non-functional save to fulfil the expectations of examination committees, and obfuscating prose as described above.

By informational redundancy I do not mean that a given
reader may already know the details of the field in question; that
is a function of the experience and knowledge of the individual.
Rather, informational redundancy comes from the common
practice of citing the obvious. Any effective informational element makes a distinctive contribution to the work in question.

But in the dissertation, accepted theses are often demonstrated and redemonstrated; time-honoured techniques are employed to their exhaustion and the readers' surfeit; redundant charts, tables, and diagrams are not only provided but discussed at length; subsidiary problems are explored which take us far afield from a tight and persuasive consideration of the argument. Redundancy weakens the surface tension of the work: it vitiates the density of information while maximizing the verbiage.

TRIVIALIZATION

It is depressing to think that the ultimate discourse in a program of graduate studies can be trivial. But one may as well face up to the fact that a dissertation that is trivial, is so *basically*; its triviality is irremediable. About all one can do with such a manuscript, aside from simply letting it rest undisturbed, is to extract from it an article or two for the learned journals. Indeed, this is precisely the advice publishers may give the writer, who too often makes his or her overture with more-than-merited optimism and insistence.

One is, however, often aware of the presence, lurking behind the dissertation, of a working mind bigger than the concepts and data in which it has been entrapped. One suspects that the writer has been victimized – by an accident of selection, by an uninspiring milieu, by poor advice, by the confidence game of the dissertation director, or by that director's personal triviality of mind. (It is only fair to balance the record by noting that excellence in works written for the degree often results from excellence of supervision.)

Trivialization thus can stem from restrictions on dissertation writers – to a topic in which they have little interest, if any at all, or to an aspect of the topic which is not as rich, challenging, or seminal as others which they are competent or disposed to deal with. In both cases trivialization may result from the dissertation writers' hireling attitude. It may also result from their lethargy. They can, as the experiences of some writers show, tailor a thesis – even if it was originally framed broadly and excitingly – to fit the data so that the dissertation is a neater package but of less consequence. In fairness it must be added that such tailoring may also occur after vigorous and exhaustive research. If the data *cannot* adequately support the thesis, the writer can only either abandon the work, which is often not feasible, or else revise the thesis to fit what data are available.

Trivialization occurs, finally, when dissertation writers fail to perceive fully the implications inherent in their research. More often than not, however, this failure is to be attributed to the next sin.

SPECIALIZATIONISM

This is a word which was expressly created to possess the heuristic value of embodying what it names – an insensitivity to language, on the one hand, and to considerations of audience, on the other. *Specializationalism* bears to *specialization* the same relation that *scientificism* (or *scientism*) bears to *science*.

It is inevitable that a dissertation should be specialized. But the question is whether in fact specialization with its concomitant limitation of communication does not sometimes become an end in itself. Specialization usually minimizes the audience. The dissertation does this efficiently since it most often remains forever unpublished, with an audience restricted to the author's most loyal friends, the examining board, and those few determined fellow-specialists who secure it from the library of deposit. For works of such limited interest, the access provided by the latter institution is wholly adequate.

But exclusion by means of ardent specialization can derive from more than the nature of the topic under investigation. There are two less natural causes – the rhetoric and the adamantly restrictive nature of the dissertation. We have perhaps devoted enough attention to the rhetoric. Let us define simply what is meant by 'adamantly restrictive nature.' I have in mind here the strong inclination of dissertation writers and directors rigorously to avoid generalization beyond the thesis itself and such 'hard evidence' as has been adduced to support it – even when it is perfectly clear that implications beyond the thesis and its data are present and clearly formulable. If, for example, a conclusion of moment to historiography is inherent in the study of a minor Renaissance court figure, or to social theory from an anthropological inquiry, to the social sciences in general from an economic study, or to the humanities from a sociological study, then why not – in the name of sanity – follow where the opportunity to generalize leads? It is likely that viewing the thesis in the broadest terms possible will give it greater value than either the writer or the director had ever thought likely. It is equally likely that its publishing history will not end in a half-dozen rejections and profound authorial despair.

REDUCTIONISM

The tendency to write about a part of a process, object, or event as though it were the whole of the phenomenon under study is, of course, reductionism. To believe that the reduction is reflective of reality and to act in terms of it – and to urge others to act in terms of it – is arrogance.

It is true that one cannot in every instance study *all* of any given phenomenon. Writers realize this; so do research directors. Even editors realize it. But to pass from the modesty of this perfectly reasonable position – because it may not fire one's imagination – and to maintain that one *can study* and indeed *has studied* all that is relevant of a process, object, or event, by means of a model, and thus to accept that model as real in its own terms, is an act of intellectual fraud. Yet this is precisely what is done, rampantly, in the humanities and the social sciences. To encourage it is shocking in disciplines which avowedly are dedicated to the study of humans-in-the-world, and which in theory at least espouse the multiplicity, the subtle and elusive complexity, and the protean inexhaustibility of human acts of being, their objects, and their events.

Reductionism is not, alas, the kind of defect which prevents a work from being published. It has been in fashion for the past few decades, and has been eagerly looked for and issued by both commercial houses and university presses. There is rich evidence, however, to indicate that its popularity is dwindling, and we may all look forward to a more honourable time when human models are recognized in terms of their limitations and are not made the measures of all things.

ARROGANCE

This is the error defined above, and it is of two kinds – the arrogance of those who know they are being arrogant, and the arrogance of those who don't. The arrogance most likely to suffuse the dissertation is of the latter kind – brassy, and without that virtuosity which sometimes accompanies conscious exploitation (for in the hands of a genius arrogance may have an *élan* that compels admiration).

I shall leave the anatomy of arrogance in general to moralists and others concerned with the diagnosis and improvement of the human character. In the dissertation, it manifests itself as a haughty resistance to change. A book can be hospitable to arrogance: it can be personal and can even, indeed, be dedicated to setting forth a banquet of piquant and enticing displays of the author's vintaged self-estimation. But a dissertation is not personal. It is supposed to be dedicated to the exposition of a thesis that is, in some sense or to some extent, true in direct relationship to the degree to which it is removed from the personality of the writer. Obviously, resistance to change on the part of the author can be inimical to the best realization of such a work.

If the dissertation is accepted for revision and publication, it is in the editorial revision that the serpent of arrogance usually bares its fangs – at the first attempt to suggest improvement. By and large, editors are accustomed to the juvenescent tantrums of neurotics. But one can hardly blame those who now and again acquiesce in rage, yielding to the temptation to permit a particularly difficult author wilfully to commit an idiocy in print. They rightly argue that such an author may as well be perceived in more than one aspect of his or her true self.

NOTE

1 *Encyclopedia Britannica* (Chicago, 1971), vol. 6, p. 111.

chapter three

Revising the Dissertation and Publishing the Book

ROBERT PLANT ARMSTRONG

Revision is not a quick rerun, a comma added here or deleted there, a bit of finishing up. As anyone who has attempted it knows, revision is a process – the process of bringing things to rights; and those who have tried it know that it is arduous, and as creative and demanding as the production of the nearly always abortive first draft. A book evolves for months, for years even, some aspect or stratum or face always in motion, becoming that which it is not yet but shows it may become. Revision requires both the ability to perceive what is unfulfilled and the energy and cunning to bring about the fulfilment. It is thus quite another process than that attention to detail which is beguiling because so easy, and which, while essential, can always, as profound and genetic matters usually cannot, be done with the help of a good editor. Revision works sea-changes in the book that none but the work can define and only the creator can perceive and bring about.

At the same time, however much a virtue revision is, it has its defect as well. The defect of revision is *constant* revision, whereby revision becomes neurotic and preventive instead of creative and liberating. An editor who encounters this neurosis should seek escape, for the neurotic writer tries to put the editor on a string: the wary editor declines to participate in so sterile a relationship.

Neurotic revisers may be the authors of one of three types of works, which I shall call security books, insecurity books, and messianic books. Perpetual revision of the first type is necessary because it is only by virtue of such works' being ever incomplete that their authors can avoid facing the judgments of their peers and possibly being found wanting. Writers of insecurity books, on the other hand, must ever postpone completion of their works because of new research they must take into account. Like all neurotics, they are geniuses at discovering such evidence as will support their inaction. Naturally, they often become enormously learned in the process and become a valuable asset to their universities even if they don't publish. Writers of messianic books are in a somewhat similar state. For them the time is not yet ripe (rather than the book); they are confident they are on the verge of discovering a principle or formulating a generalization which will restructure their disciplines and earn them the fame for which they have so long waited. Writers of messianic books are, furthermore, doubtful whether any publisher has the perspicacity to comprehend or value them fully.

Once in a great while a foolish editor or colleague will pry loose from its author the messianic book, or the insecurity book, or the security book. When this happens, both editor (or helpful colleague) and author will live to regret it. The editor discovers a nemesis – the author who is forever changing the text, who quibbles over design, and who visits all his or her frustrations upon the editor. What is more, upon publication of the book such authors often find their worst suspicions justified – the book is ill received and they hate themselves, their colleagues, the reviewers, the editor, the publisher, and the system. Far better they had spent the rest of their lives revising.

Yet *revision* is a marvellous word. It means re-seeing the work; and the -*vision* part of it suggests more than mere seeing. 'Vision' can connote perception of the ideal and imply a marvel. Thus *revision* may truly be called a marvellous word. It is also an optimistic word, for to re-vision the work and shape it more closely toward the ideal attests to the viability of the creative principle in *homo faber*. At the same time, *revision* is elusive, for it is unique with each writer confronting the first draft. It is as profound a process as the author is profound, as subtle as he or she is subtle, and therefore, inscrutable. Thus no program of simple or even difficult steps can be described in working a revision. It is possible, however, to make a few observations that generally apply.

Some of the aspects of revision can be discussed under the rubrics of the three prime virtues of the book: probity, responsibility, and unity.

REVISION FOR PROBITY

The basic concern of the writer of the dissertation (having won his or her degree) is to ascertain whether in fact the proper thesis has been developed, for the thesis that met the requirements of the dissertation may not be at all adequate for the book. The thesis director may, indeed, have shunted the author into an alternative and less important path. Now there is the chance to revise the work, to reinstate the original thesis and eliminate the one incorporated into the dissertation for the purpose of securing a Ph.D.

But the real thesis can be lost in other ways or it may be that the writer never found the thesis that should have been asserted throughout the inquiry, in which event even after revision a bad book will result, if any book results at all. It may be the author's own obtuseness that occludes the probity and authenticity of the work. Or the author may have succumbed to one of the tyrannical conceptual fads. Whatever the cause, the result is the same: a potentially meaningful work is aborted.

The author is probably fortunate, if hardly laudable, if the thesis has been consciously perverted for pragmatic ends. Under this circumstance revision is relatively simple. Otherwise, finding the hidden thesis – or, even anterior to that, discerning that there is a crypto-thesis – can be difficult. In any event, given that the dissertation is based on an inapposite thesis, the first and most important job of revision is to identify the right one.

If the dissertation has not been wilfully misdirected, then there is a strong possibility that the author will not recognize that it contains the wrong thesis. Yet such a writer may not be hopelessly lost – what may be required for extrication is only the slightest lead. The moral is obvious: even if one thinks one's work is ever so good, the candid opinions of those whom one respects are of value. Candid opinions are, however, rare.

A trial separation of the writer from the work (a final divorcement often happens at this point) is essential under all circumstances. Then a leisurely return is in order, reconstructing the work in one's mind, playing with the thesis as a conceptual sport, testing it for fullness and further applicability. Finally, the writer achieves enough distance from the dissertation that he or she can look at it dispassionately, and make an uncompromising evaluation: how does this work compare in weight and significance, in probity, with the important theses of the discipline, and, if it fails to measure up, is it true that the work is negligible or did it somehow drift into inconsequentiality through misdirection, lethargy, lack of control, absence of ability, or the sway of fashion? At this point it is perhaps well to examine the progress of the work, from beginning to end, in order to see if it is possible to gain hold of any loose ends, or pattern of loose ends, which will lead back to that confounding of errors which has grown into major misdirection, a misdirection which has through its ever-compounding course created a different work. Indeed, if at any point a clever argument has taken over from the author – which is a much less mysterious occurrence than it might seem – let the author be deeply suspicious.

The identification of the right thesis can proceed by such methods of triangulation. When the sensitive writer – and it is 'sensitive' which is the ineluctable term in these formulations – sights the lost thesis, he or she will feel a shock of recognition that reverberates with unmistakable authority.

The most basic task of revision is this recognition; all else depends upon it. The other points to be considered are, however, important, because they maximize the values implicit in good work.

We have noted that revision is a process. For that matter a book is itself a process, and so must its chief virtues and aspects be. Probity is a process and as a process it exists in time. As a temporal continuum it is subject to dynamics, and it is in the various modulations of the work that revision can be most creative and rewarding.

Pertinence, consequence, and seriousness of purpose must be ever-present in the work, but they need not pervade it with maximum intensity. A book pulsates – it has systoles and diastoles – and from these we infer its vitality. The book's pulses derive from alternate intensifying and relaxation of the three aspects of probity. Like a person, the book grows more intense and more serious, and its acts become of greater consequence and pertinence, as it draws nearer to critical points. And like a person under such circumstances, its breath comes faster, its whole physiology is speeded up. This variation of pace and this modulation can be achieved by the writer in the process of revision. Herein lies the writer's artistry. Sensitivity – heightening of knowledge, giving it an affective dimension – imagination, and the skill to plot and execute the dynamics of probity that are perceived are the writer's sole allies in bringing the work to life.

The dissertation will require more and more arduous labours in pursuit of these simple dynamics than will the work that was written in the first place to be a book. At the same time, it is the abashed writer of the dissertation who will be most bewildered by this advice. It would be easy to warn the dissertation writer not to try, but as a publisher I know well that the talent which takes longest to burst into flame sometimes finally burns the brightest. Therefore I can but advise dissertation writers to read the best writers of their respective disciplines and their day with an awareness tuned to the measures and techniques by means of which the modulations of dynamics are achieved.

What we have called modulation is clearly a linear dynamic; but there is a lateral, or synchronic, dynamic as well. Therefore it is also during the process of revision that the 'mix' between inquiry and demonstration (which in the dissertation is the act of fulfilling degree requirements by means of rhetorical and structural clichés) may be adjusted. The book mix should be very rich indeed in inquiry, anaemic in demonstration. In the first reading after the post-dissertational fallow period its authenticity will reveal the quality of the former, while its counterfeiture will reveal the latter.

But not only this mix should be adjusted in the revision. There is also the word-idea ratio, as well as all the other aspects of synchronic structure. And the adjustment will be not for probity alone, but also for unity, for responsibility, and for style. Careful, unrelenting control over synchronic mix will produce a taut and pertinent continuum in the discourse – a continuum which, vital with diachronic modulations, will go far toward achieving a good book.

REVISION FOR RESPONSIBILITY

The revision of the work for responsibility is to move it fully from inquisition – in which the subject matter is tortured to death, its vitals strewn among inimical forms, inept techniques, and babbling notes – to inquiry which constitutes itself through words complete in all forms, fibres, and functions. The procreative task of the writer in the revision is to create the work in words, carefully endowing it with germs of wholeness, fullness, and geneticity so that layer by layer, process by process, structure by structure, it becomes an organism.

The writer may well bear in mind during the re-reading the remarkable extent to which the serious book of non-fiction resembles the novel. That novel whose scene is not built to functional adequacy, whose characters are automatons, and whose acts are without credibility is a novel which lacks responsibility in the sense in which we have been using the term. The novelist must create a whole organism out of that organism's own parts. The world of the novel is thus constituted in believability. The same holds true of the scholarly work. It makes no difference that the one work deals with an imagined drama of the interactions of invented humans and the other with descriptions of or inventions about human existence or the real or hypothetical world. The obligation to create full-dimensional believability is as incumbent upon the writer of non-fiction as it is upon the writer of novels.

The inclusion of encyclopaedic detail does not achieve free-standingness in the scholarly book any more than it does in the novel. Indeed, as even the most patient reader knows, massive detail is tiresome and confusing; it smothers the work, makes it diffuse, and defeats the objective. Detail must be chosen with a clear sense of its significance *to the constitution of a whole and elegant organism*. Wholeness does not mean exhaustiveness; exhaustiveness yields exhaustion. It is for this reason that publishers reject a groaning weight of absolute documentation, abject demonstration, and utter datafication.

Thus the process of revision provides prolix writers with the opportunity to carve away at the grossness of their work and anaemic writers to add to theirs – both with the purpose of portraying *in line* tissues, processes, and structures. A responsible work is like a responsible bridge – a function of all the fibres and tensions it requires to exist as bridge. Decorations are not only baroque: they may jeopardize the possibility that the work will endure.

REVISION FOR UNITY

Presumably a successful dissertation has achieved that minimal unity of demonstration that broods like an ungainly but all-powerful tyrant over the good data, good thought, and good intentions it has usurped. At the same time it has achieved an acceptable degree of focus, which doubtless substitutes for genuine fixity. With these two pseudo-unities the dissertation may be submitted, and the degree secured.

But we know that the object of unity is to achieve a *genetic* unity in all strata of the work. Genetic unity is unity of thesis, unity of inquiry through the unities of probity and responsibility. These all add up to a *wholeness* of the work such that it becomes a fulfilled and fulfilling phenomenon energized with its inherent system of energies.

The achievement of wholeness results from the ever-growing mastery of the writer over the work. He or she succeeds in moulding together all aspects and faces so that they cohere and have plasticity, so that the work takes its natural, inevitable, and therefore most elegant form.

There is much more that ought to be said about revision and yet so little that can be said. I shall not even begin to speak of style, leaving that to the writer and to his or her external super-ego, the editor. I turn, instead, to the act of publishing.

PUBLICATION

A book is a verbal creation giving a perspective on human experience and the world. It is also a contribution to the sum of values, views, and attitudes that comprise the nature of human existence in a given era, and shape its view of the cosmos. The greatest books establish perspectives that win belief and thus endure for generations, for centuries, or even for millennia. All this is in the nature of the book. But not until it is published. Publication is the natural end of the book; but it is not the natural end of the dissertation. The natural end of the dissertation is reached when the committee accepts it and the degree is granted. The dissertation is not a fact in the world of facts, but only a fact of the author's education. The publisher is more aware of this than most academics, who, having directed their students in writing dissertations, advise them to submit these works to publishers; so it is that many publishers categorically decline to consider dissertations.

But the establishment of fact is a social prerogative. And so it follows that validation and objectification of the literary work is usually placed in the hands of the publisher whom the economics of success have confirmed as society's executor of its literary powers. Publishing is therefore to be seen as a normative activity that operates to define and maintain ideas, forms, and standards of discourse. The implications of this fact are enormous indeed, for in these terms publishing becomes on the one hand a dynamic of communications stability, and on the other an institutionalized inhibition upon the erratic and chaotic development of literary forms.

The normative characteristics of publishing do not result from a capricious coalition of editors, however. Publishing persists by virtue of a kind of social contract among publishers, writers, and readers. Further, changes in the forms of communication (as opposed to the various *means* of communication, which change rapidly) tend to be slow. But it would be a disservice to the understanding of publishing if one were to permit the matter to stand at this, for it is clear that publishing is both positive and innovative – positive in the sense that it tends in the long run to be subject to historical changes, operating in accordance with the interests and practices of the day; and innovative in the sense that it often undertakes to incorporate in its processes a wide range of textual and structural mutations. It is clear, however, that such innovation is more likely to be found in the forms of fiction, verse, and interpretive non-fiction than in the scholarly book as we know it.

Only the most ardent determinist sees publishing solely as a process that inevitably expresses impersonal social forces. The more experienced observers recognize that it is infinitely personal as well, that individuals have profoundly and significantly shaped book publishing – notably, in trade publishing, Alfred A. Knopf. To name a similarly important person in university publishing – one who by his or her personality and taste helped shape an industry – is not possible, owing to the existence of the factor of university control which tends to minimize the more individualistic aspects of the publisher's role and to collectivize the interpretation of the functions of publishing, the character of the list, and the nature of the scholarship which goes to create that list.

The publisher as agent of society in publishing a book causes the latter to define its time not only for its author's day, but for the future as well. The publisher is thus the agent of history, and the author's book the projection of the author into the trajectory of history. It is as an effective delineator of the shape of current times and as an arbiter of history that the publisher completes the work of the author.

Publishers as the agents of these events are thus placed in a position of considerable power, and their obligations are accordingly very great. The best publishers are therefore those who are dedicated, through personal faith, to the most creative social ends – university publishers generally to long-term ends, and commercial publishers generally, though by no means exclusively, to those more immediate ones in which they are specialists, the satisfaction of which requires strategic contemporaneity of book and immediacy of sale.

But if publishers are not merely slaves to the historical process, it does not follow that they are without a sense of the sociality of their actions and of their responsibility for them. There are many significant evidences of publishers' response in this respect, though we shall here mention but one, an evidence so basic to the publishing presence, however, as necessarily to become involved in any discussion of the nature of publishing. I am thinking of the dedication of various publishing houses to the development in depth of one or several specific disciplines or arts. Thus publishers may serve history by virtue of the fact that they can direct the present, rather than merely rest content with reinforcing its values and practices.

But whether development- or service-oriented, publishing is definitive, adding by means of its strong strokes to the sharp delineation of the form and feature of its time. When authors submit their works to a publisher, they enter into the historical process in a way that is more direct, immediate, and (save perhaps for producing children) more personal and irrevocable than all the other actions of their lives. They have good reason therefore subsequently to have anxieties more compelling than those of mere waiting. They know that now they must be prepared to go into history and to present themselves at their best.

Their work is about to be judged for its probity, unity, and responsibility; its graces and its elegance; and its potentiality as a charge of energy induced into the accrued force of their epoch.

If the prospect of entering history is overwhelming – or unrealistic – and the possibility of contributing to the more or less ephemeral dialogue of one's day seems more probable, even so the publisher as an agent of society must legitimize the work, promising through the authority of its imprint that the work at least conforms to the nature of a book and deserves to be published. For the book for the day is no less a book than the book for the ages – it is only mortal rather than immortal. Its mortality is inherent in its thesis, the measure of its probity, its contemporaneity, and its restricted commitment to history and to universality.

No matter whether the work is to endure or soon to vanish, publication is the instrument of the processes of history, not only in creating the public record and content of a literary and intellectual history, but also in selecting and building those literary events which are to be the history of the epoch. No mere agent of tradition, then, but its generator, the publisher bears a final and awesome relationship to the writer's book.

Given the social and historical nature of the act of publishing, it is not surprising that the process of bringing the book into being should be as normative as the original act of selection. Thus both in the editing and in the designing of the book, the canons of the best language and the best appearance are invoked to make the book a product of its day. In most American publishing houses, two different kinds of editors are ordinarily involved in the process of turning the author's work into a printed book. The one with whom the writer initially engages, the acquisitions or sponsoring editor, makes the first expression of interest; if he or she likes the work and wishes it to be published, it is presented to the head of the house with the editor's recommendation. Prior to this, of course, the work has been read by the acquisitions editor and sent to specialist readers for criticism. If in the acquisitions editor's judgment their opinions warrant proceeding, he or she urges publication.

It is this editor who will recommend to the author those major revisions he or she and the specialist readers deem necessary or desirable. Often this occurs prior to the offering of a contract, although not always. The work is, of course, the author's, and the decision to accept or reject the recommended changes is the author's as well. But the money is the publisher's, and if the writer is reluctant to make the suggested changes, the publisher may not be willing to proceed with the negotiations and may not offer a contract. If the publisher has sufficient confidence in the work, however, it may decide to go along on the writer's terms.

After the questions of major revision have been adjudicated, the manuscript is placed in the hands of the manuscript editor, with whom the writer may expect a prolonged relationship of considerable intimacy – an intimacy both professional and personal, both intellectual and emotional. The editor reads the work more carefully and (if this is not too great a paradox to contemplate) with greater *detached empathy* than either the author's friends or enemies subsequently will. The editor learns the work habits of the writer's mind, its strengths and its shortcomings, those short cuts it is likely to seek and the turgid prolixities it may sometimes like to effect when it knows but won't admit it is not going any place. The manuscript editor evaluates and exploits the writer's talents, to the end of helping the writer to mobilize *all* his or her resources, so that the very best book possible can be produced.

And yet, *mirabile dictu*, the good manuscript editor achieves so much without stridency. That this is so is sometimes a monument to human endurance with dignity, for unfortunately some authors are insolent without cause, arrogant with no justification, proud of their misuse of the English language, and intemperate in their satisfaction with their own abilities. Fortunately, such traits are frequently visible from afar and, barring the major work of genius, small attention need be paid to the antics – which often are excessive in direct ratio to the mediocrity of the work. A good manuscript editor, being more long-suffering than the writer of this article, would very likely not have written the above. I do it gratuitously on that editor's behalf. Some bold soul must set the record straight!

But the time comes when both author's and editor's options are limited. The work is brought into final form. Now the book is neither the author's nor the publisher's; it becomes its own, its free-standingness finally achieved. It is now sent to the designer.

The design of the book, too, is normative, in the sense that it reflects the designer's idea of how a book of the kind ought to look. At the same time, however, it is also positive in that it reflects the day's prevailing aesthetics of design, and, indeed, the *weltgefühl* of its period. Design is more subject to rapid change than editorial practices, as may be seen by comparing the two features in books from the 1920s, for example, with those of today. A further consideration must be borne in mind as well, namely, that design is an expressive dimension, not only of the taste of the age but also of the content of the book. Design thus rounds out the act of pre-emption which the epoch asserts upon its books – as it does indeed upon all its other productions as well – and the designer quite as clearly and as decisively as the acquisitions and manuscript editors executes the dictates of society and makes a contribution to history. The cut of the typeface (whether linear or cursive, with or without serifs), the style of designing a page (open or tight, with or without wide margins), the setting of the lines to execute this design, the finish and the colour of the paper – all these variables express the prevailing taste. Design at its best also expresses the particularity of the book, the designer using both the visual properties of the type and the degree of interlinear and intercharacter space to express such aspects of the text as its conformity or its freedom, its gravity or its superficiality, its propriety or its irreverence.

Yet if I portray publishers only as agents of abstract social forces, I am being a simple-minded determinist. Culture, society, and history all move upon multiple feet, like a horrendous and mutated millipede whose countless feet are the untold humans who constitute it. Publishers work with the particular books of particular authors, and good publishers never forget the human rootedness of the books they publish. They know that they produce self-sustaining surrogates for the author, and that no matter how much the book may become divorced from the person – even though the author should be or through time should become anonymous – yet the publisher knows it is a particular voice that speaks. The publisher does not forget, therefore, that the ultimate term constituting the personal equation in publishing is the discrete work of a particular author. Though inexorably acting out the grand designs of social forces, good publishers never subordinate their authors to considerations of a vast and impersonal social design. They realize that in the final analysis the act of publishing is the act of publishing a person, whose work is his or her personal and intellectual odyssey. Although on publication of the work the publisher causes it to be divorced from the author, as mother is divorced at birth from child, yet does the publisher know that the author has still to enjoy the pride of creation that comes from seeing the work take its place in the dynamic of its discipline and its day.

chapter four

Avoiding the Warmed-Over Dissertation

WILLIAM C. DOWLING

In her essay in this volume, Francess G. Halpenny remarks, '... a scholarly work of analysis or criticism should impart to the reader the writer's conviction that the subject is worth writing about' – a point from which a beginning scholar can only derive comfort. The path a junior scholar travels in reaching this same conclusion, however, is not so comfortable, and I remember my own anxieties years ago, when I hadn't yet begun to rewrite my doctoral dissertation as a book. The concerns of a young Ph.D. are not at that moment Olympian, and the question, as one sits at a desk with two bound copies of one's dissertation, is distressingly practical: 'Very well, but *how*?'

When I began to think about writing a book, a curious thing happened: I found myself turning over the pages of scholarly works I'd known for years, and some which I'd never have opened otherwise, with a new and critical eye – looking for models. And here the practical worries began: the classics, which were of course the works to emulate, were almost always written by seasoned scholars in their intellectual prime; they were inspiring, but at the moment impossible as models. But then, sitting in great profusion on the shelves of my local bookstore, were all the others: books which were not books at all but warmed-over dissertations – precisely the kind of thing one is determined not to write.

The warmed-over dissertation will some day, I hope, be regarded as an embarrassing episode in the history of scholarly publishing, recalling the unwary exuberance of university presses. But the young Ph.D., determined to make that first book a real contribution to the field, is unlikely to take comfort in any long-term historical perspective, for the immediate concern is to avoid the genre altogether. The central question, once again, is severely practical: what distinguishes the warmed-over dissertation from the genuine scholarly book which happens to have its origin in research undertaken for a dissertation?

My bookstore research, casual as it was, seemed to suggest at least one useful distinction: the genuine book is an elaboration of a single significant idea, and the warmed-over dissertation isn't. To borrow Robert Plant Armstrong's phrase, the warmed-over dissertation is a 'non-thesis book,' and its author, working without a strong central conception, cannot hope to solve such problems with revision.

There are a number of easily observed features, I found, which distinguish the thesis book from the non-thesis one. In my own field (literary criticism), the warmed-over dissertation is almost certain to have a fancy non-descriptive main title (*The Naked Dreamer: A Study of James Joyce*) and a battery of epigraphs at the beginning of each new chapter; its text will consist of a plodding succession of commentary and quotes, quotes and commentary. The non-introduction to a non-thesis book provides either a perfunctory review-of-scholarship-on-the-subject or an incoherent bill of fare ('While my main concern is with X, I have attempted to deal also with Y, and have glanced briefly at Z'). Here are some phrases gleaned from one such introduction:

Although I do not actually conclude that ...
I am basically more concerned with ...
My own interest is in ... though I also deal with ...
But even though I will generalize in this area, I will not devote
    myself to ...
In contrast to most critics of ____, I argue that ...

> The heart of my interest is in ...
> Because of this emphasis I can refer only fittingly if at all to ...

The dilemma of the author without an argument is implicit in these phrases, and they provide a perfect illustration of what the young scholar contemplating the first book wishes to avoid. To me, this seemed to suggest an obvious starting point for a systematic approach to rewriting: since the warmed-over dissertation is a monograph in belated search of an idea, the process should probably begin with the question 'Do I really have an idea?'

Once I brought myself to the point of asking this question, I remember, it became less dismaying than it sounds: there surely couldn't be anything very ignoble in coming to the honest conclusion that I hadn't said anything immensely significant in the dissertation, and turning my energies to writing separate essays on the two or three more important points I'd developed. But after several long evenings in my office, rereading the dissertation and drinking coffee and trying to be as objective as possible, I decided that I'd been lucky – somewhere in there, hidden in a tangle of notes and commentary and digressions, was a reasonably promising main idea.

At this point came another painful moment of self-examination: was that main idea important enough to justify a full-length study? If it wasn't, I decided, my best option was the same as before: I'd have material for a major article but not for a book, and my effort had best go into writing a polished and soundly developed essay. After a few more nights of coffee and solitude, though, it did seem as though the idea might be worth pursuing for two or three hundred pages, and I began thinking about the next step.

The next step, which surprised me when I finally got to it, was to write the introduction. Since the introduction to every non-thesis book I looked at gave the impression of being an afterthought, a last-ditch attempt to justify a work with no real argument, it seemed clear that the author of a book with an important point to make should use the introduction to present this main idea clearly and compellingly, and to awaken the reader's interest in the detailed discussion to follow. The introduction to a thesis book, it seemed to me, should stand almost as an essay in itself, except that it would be full of points that begged for further elaboration.

That, at any rate, was the theory. When I actually sat down to write, I admit that I found the whole prospect somewhat intimidating – the first thirty pages of my dissertation were a hopeless example of the muddled non-introduction, and I soon realized that I'd embarked on a new and fairly demanding project. But in the next month or so, as my introduction took shape, I became more and more convinced that I'd chosen the right course.

The best reason for writing the introduction first, I discovered, was eminently practical: it compels you to refine your argument at the beginning of revision, when it's most essential to do so. Since you've already done a dissertation on your subject, there's little danger of straying into unsupported generalization, and the introduction becomes a place where you can develop the broader implications of your main concept at the same time as you introduce it.

The final step, of course, is to rewrite everything else. Once again, my experience has confirmed the practical wisdom of beginning with the introduction. If the introduction is an honest and competent piece of work, the benefits begin to appear immediately: with a firm sense of direction, you have little trouble realigning your original insights with your major point, getting rid of smothering documentation and digressive or irrelevant material, and (one hopes) gracefully subordinating the particular to the general. When the rewriting is finished, there is some reason to hope that it is the rough draft not of a warmed-over dissertation but of a book.

A rough draft is only that, of course, and there are still visions and revisions (about five revisions) to come, and even then there's no guarantee that the manuscript is publishable, or that any publisher will take it. But the experience of trying to write a genuinely thoughtful and learned work, it seems to me, is indispensable for anyone seriously committed to scholarship, and carries its own reward. That was once the rationale behind the doctoral dissertation, and even now, when the dissertation has become an empty ritual, it is a sound one.

One final observation: Robert Plant Armstrong argues that 'there is every reason why, in this day of Ph.D. overproduction, the requirement to write a dissertation should be dropped and the requirement to write a book substituted.'[1] Armstrong's solution is a good one: if a new-model car shows a high incidence of brake failure, we do not conclude that the manufacturer should stop putting brakes into its automobiles, but that better ones should be installed. Armstrong is implicitly arguing, it seems to me, for a total reform of graduate education, one that would reinstate the Ph.D. as a symbol of scholarly and intellectual competence, and would attract to the academic profession only the people who are fitted for it by talent and commitment. This is the only answer: the widespread unease among publishers, readers, graduate schools, and young scholars concerning the doctoral dissertation is real, but it is mostly the dissatisfaction of people who don't know why they're doing what they're doing, and who are unhappily convinced that it is too late to change.

NOTE

1 Robert Plant Armstrong, 'The Qualities of a Book, the Wants of a Dissertation,' in *The Thesis and the Book*, 1st ed., ed. Eleanor Harman and Ian Montagnes (Toronto: University of Toronto Press, 1976), 26.

chapter five

Thesis to Book: What to Get Rid of and What to Do with What Is Left

OLIVE HOLMES

PART I

The art of communication is one of the arts of survival for scholars. If they take seriously the command to 'publish or perish,' writing well becomes a matter of life and death. Scholars are not, therefore, in a mood of confident relaxation when they approach that blank page, and this anxiety may be responsible for some of the common defects of academic writing.

The first book manuscript prepared by the beginning academic writer is very often the Ph.D. thesis, which is submitted to a publisher either as it stands or following substantial revision. In making the suggestions that follow, I am not recommending this practice nor am I against it. I am aware that some writers of Ph.D. theses are quite content to have their work remain in that category and have no great desire to publish a book. I am also aware that some theses are so well written that they do not need much further editing to become publishable. Nor do I equate a thesis with poor writing and a book with good writing, or suggest that one is necessarily inferior to the other. The point is that a thesis and a book are different. If scholars understand this difference, they are more apt to wind up with a publishable manuscript.

A thesis is written to display knowledge, to persuade, and to impress. It is written for a specific reward – a degree, and for a specific audience – a committee of specialists. It is a demonstration of the writer's ability to handle research as well as a report on a particular subject, and is involved with method as well as content. Since it is a test of a certain kind of expertise, it falls into the category of examination with all the emphasis on how well the student performs. Content is more important than communication, and the author (and his or her ability) more important than either.

The purpose of a book is quite different. A book is primarily a communication, whether it is about the control of aphids or T'ang sculpture, the Dead Sea Scrolls or the Pentagon Papers. A book in some cases is indeed a performance, but it exists apart from its author as a child exists apart from its parents. The reader is not primarily interested in the author but in the book.

A book does not talk to itself but discloses something to someone. Authors of books concentrate on getting their ideas across rather than making an impression. In so doing, they shift their attention from themselves to the work at hand. They set aside their personal goals and reach out to make their ideas clear to others. Paradoxically, they will be more objective while putting more of themselves into their work. Since much of good writing comes out of the ends of the fingers, authors of books now have to use more of their subconscious minds, which, in their preoccupation with rational thinking, they may have ignored. They are, in effect, now adding art to scholarship in order to communicate fully. Many scholars are culture-bound in the sense that their concentration on the purely intellectual has caused them to denigrate feeling. Even a feeling for words sometimes seems to them to be faintly orgiastic.

A book, then, is not a warmed-over or patched-up thesis. The evolution from one to the other demands a whole new approach, a different way of looking at the material, of envisioning the reader, and even a new motivation. The author of a thesis is still a student; in trying to turn the thesis into a book, he or she becomes a writer with obligations to a reader. The reader is the person to be reckoned with, not as judge and jury, but as someone to be informed, to be enlightened, even to be rescued, for as E.B. White, relaying the words of his teacher, has written: 'Will [Strunk] felt that the reader was in serious trouble most of the time, a man floundering in a swamp, and that it was the duty of anyone attempting to write English to drain this swamp quickly and get this man up on dry ground, or at least throw him a rope.'[1] Thesis writers are not concerned about throwing a rope to their doctoral committee; indeed, they are hoping the committee will fling one to them. But as book authors, their attitude has to change to one of tender consideration for the person floundering in the swamp. If thesis writers can make this mental shift, they are on their way to becoming writers of books. They might even find that their efforts lead them into a maturing and invigorating experience.

The Trumpeter Effect

The first step in the transformation of a thesis into a book is to get rid of the signs of a thesis. This is essentially a negative process, but it has to come first.

The most common of these signs is the 'trumpeter effect' or 'bulletin-board announcement.' So accustomed are thesis writers to the blackboard background that they tend to interrupt themselves by posting notices. They never quite manage to live in the present of their work – only in its past and the future. There is consequently a lot of pointing out, reminding, and referring – signposts which intelligent readers resent. For example:

This chapter will deal with the first period of the Cordovan Caliphate. The second period will be dealt with in the following chapter ...

In a later section of this chapter further information will be presented to elaborate on the question of the value of the click beetle as predator ...

It is also unnecessary to tell captive readers what they have just read. Presumably they are not spot-checking the book. The author hopes and should assume that every word will be read, even though this is probably optimistic. (A scholarly writer might as well be resigned to the fact that every word of the book may not and probably will not be read, particularly if it has a good index – that boon to the busy academic.) In any event, there is no need to remind readers what the last chapter was about:

> The August seventh agenda of the Steering Committee of the Society for the Suppression of Pornographic Literature has already been analyzed in my last chapter.

> Most of the relevant changes in the relations between the third assistant secretary and the leader of the Youth Caucus have been illustrated in a discussion of other issues in our first two chapters. See also Appendix Yc.

Sometimes an author not only backtracks but announces that there is no need to. For example, the author may claim: 'There should be no need to recapitulate the factors' which led up to the outbreak of the Civil War or the settlement of the railroad strike or which entered into the decision to turn his or her thesis into a book. The reader is tempted to reply: 'Then don't!' The trouble with all this forewarning and recapitulating is that it makes the reader feel like a spectator seated near the centre line at a tennis match or like a guest speaker forced to sit through a business meeting of the Women's Auxiliary of the Society for the Preservation of the Cyrus P. Titherington Homestead before being permitted to begin the address. The announcements of meeting times and places, of postponements, acknowledgments, and arrangements are not in the realm of either speech-making or literature and must simply be got through. The mind, in fact, wanders. That may be exciting at a tennis match, or endurable for the members at a business meeting, but is ruinous for a book. If the reader's mind wanders, the author may never get it back again.

One reason for this tendency to see-saw between past and future is that most writers of theses are also teachers or, as students, have been long exposed to teaching techniques including advance warning and repetition. Teachers often point out what the next lesson is going to be, and review the last one. They may do so to remind the absent-minded student that there are lesson assignments and ignorance of them is no excuse; but the habit becomes a part of teachers' equipment and creeps into their writing, even for peers. Repetition is a deliberate technique in the classroom, but less desirable in books. Readers are not smarter and not necessarily more wide awake than students, but they do have the advantage of having all the words in one place where they can look forward or back at will. News commentators may feel they need to recap the top story for the benefit of latecomers in their audience. But this is not a worry for authors. (They have many others to make up for it.) The audience of one reader has been there all the time.

When authors put up signposts, they are talking down. They are saying to the reader, in effect: 'You can't really do this on your own. You need a guided tour. Let me take you by the hand.' But the most compelling reason for cutting out all these announcements is that they are a dead give-away that the author's work is still in thesis form. The outline is showing through.

The outline, which helped to organize the author's thoughts, should now disappear. The artist conceals her art. The painter does not exhibit his preliminary sketches (unless he is a Picasso). The first draft of the Declaration of Independence, on exhibit in the Library of Congress, is a reminder of the universal human tendency to stumble in and out of sentences. Since there are few Picassos or Jeffersons among us, it would seem best to delete those first tentative efforts and forget them. An outline is only a thinking aid, not an end.

Writers of books should now seek to draw attention, not to themselves and to their worthiness as degree candidates, but to their subject. One of the most effective and quickest ways to achieve this step forward is to search the manuscript for moments when, in the words of Emerson, the author 'postpones or remembers,' and eliminate them. Living in the present, highly recommended for everyone by Emerson, is a particular virtue in a writer.

The Apologetic Opening

Closely related to the trumpeter effect is the apologetic opening. It is a limp cousin to the hyperactive forewarning and summing up. There is an excruciating false modesty about the preface that plunges immediately into an explanation of what the author has not done, giving lengthy reasons. There is also a great misunderstanding of the reader's reactions. First impressions are important. If the author sidles up to the subject and then starts moving crabwise over a host of negative statements, it is a patient reader indeed who will bother to go further. The reaction is, if the author has not done all this, what in the world did he or she do?

> Although I do not feel that I have covered the ground that should have been covered, because of the paucity of sources, an attempt has been made, however, to bring out certain aspects of the subject which have seemingly, although not entirely, some foundation. Consequently, there are large areas which have not been touched upon. I must also point out that there are some doubts about the authenticity of the Granville Documents and I tend to share the conclusions of some authors who believe that they are entirely suspect. I was also not able to spend all the time I would have liked to in the family archives of Englebert, Lord Pricklypear, for reasons which I shall not go into here.

And so on, and on. At the end of this chronicle of non-accomplishment and self-doubt, one wonders what can possibly be contained in the six to eight hundred pages that follow. One is not inclined to try to find out.

It does not seem possible that the above example could be made more apologetic, but some authors transcend it by stating that they are not going to be apologetic – which has the peculiar effect of a crab scuttling diagonally backwards:

> Instead of offering a long apology for choosing this topic, I should like at the outset to delimit the subject of this book ... I shall not predict the future nor shall I talk about the crucial problem of the relationship between ... I have to ignore the important question ...

This is a kind of trumpeter effect in reverse as well as an apologetic substitute for an apology, all of which adds up to a most effective device to 'delimit' the reader's interest.

The necessity to explain oneself is, of course, a thesis hangover, a piece of self-consciousness, which should be discarded. The non-professional reader cheerfully assumes that if the author is writing a book, then probably there are some good reasons for it, not the least of which is that the author has something to say. It is not really necessary to go into the whys and wherefores too deeply, unless these are special or peculiar. If a book is about living in a commune in the South African bush, the reader might perhaps be interested in how the author happened on the topic. But normally the reader will expect the author simply to go ahead and tell whatever story he or she has to tell.

Is the scholarly book different in this matter? No. The research for it has usually, although not always, been carried out in libraries, and an explanation may sometimes be required of how the facts were obtained. Otherwise one may be guilty of the vice of the unsupported statement – true. But these are matters best confined to the back matter. A note at the head of the bibliography can be useful when the author feels compelled to explain.

I've never known a scholar yet who was not conscious of some deficiencies when writing a book, but an introduction is not the place to dwell upon them. One should not cease being genuinely modest and aware of how much remains to be done, but it is better to look on the bright side at what has been accomplished in relation to this book, and give oneself, and the reader, a break. Life is short, art and scholarship are long. It's the finished product that matters in both of the latter, not the sketches and skirmishes. When the product is good, there is no need to apologize for it. If it is not, no amount of apology will make it any better. A book stands on its own.

Ghostly Colleagues

Some theses give the impression that their authors wrote them in a crowded study with a number of their colleagues peeking over their shoulders making comments. Such authors, unfortunately, become self-conscious in the presence of so many of their peers or of those who have gone before them. It is a bit like having ancestors glaring down from the portraits on the walls.

The nature of scholarship is to build on the work of others, and rightly so, and the work of others must be acknowledged. Again it is not a question of either/or but of how much. A thesis, far more than a book, will normally mention the work of others, either to agree or to disagree with them. Sometimes this kind of thing gets into internecine academic feuds with which the general reader has no patience. The specialist may be interested to know that La Flamme's theories, first expounded in 1899, were superseded by Von Humpack's in 1905, and that nothing of any great value had been done in this area of research until the present author overturned both La Flamme and Von Humpack by a brilliant diagnosis of the nature of their fallacies and a complete exposure of their mistakes. But to most potential readers this is footnote information, not the main thrust of the work, a sideshow that sometimes can be pretty interesting but most of the time is a great bore.

I am not suggesting that the contributions of others be ignored, only that they be put in their proper place with a proper emphasis. They can be interruptive, and when pushed to an extreme they throw the book off balance into a discussion of other people's work. A book crowded with the ghosts of the author's scholarly ancestors creaks like a haunted house.

In his delightful spoof, *The Pooh Perplex*, Frederick C. Crews

parodies such academic sparring in a chapter entitled 'Paradox-
ical Persona: The Hierarchy of Heroism in Winnie-the-Pooh,' by
a mythical Harvey C. Windrow:

> It is, then, with a sense of my own temerity – if not indeed, of out-
> right rashness – that I must assert that Ogle, Smythe, Bunker, and
> Wart have completely missed the point of Pooh. Valuable as their
> studies have been in establishing certain connections and parallels
> that other scholars might not have thought were worth pursuing, I
> cannot honestly say that we have learned anything significant
> from them. Neither Ogle, nor Smythe, nor Bunker, nor Wart asked
> himself the absolutely basic questions about Winnie-the-Pooh,
> and thus each of them necessarily failed to grasp the key to the
> book's entire meaning. I find myself in the embarrassing position
> of being the only possessor of this key, and I am writing this essay
> only to alter such an unbalanced situation as quickly as possible.[2]

The social scientists argue that their work is different from the
historian's and literary critic's and this is partly true. They claim
that they are more concerned with methodology than the historian, that because they are still working out approaches and sys-
tems, the mechanics of their research is an important subject.
They are still, as I understand it, absorbed in their own technique. This need not mean, however, that the author should not
try to get beyond a limitation (and this absorption in methodology is a limitation, as far as clarity and readability are concerned) to the happy land where technique is subordinate to
communication.

The Warm-Up Period

The first four or five pages of a first draft are, more often than
not, dispensable. Ask authors or editors where they look first
for cuts and they will probably answer that the beginning of a
manuscript offers the greatest chance of compression. The reason is simple. We tend to go through a warm-up period, a time
of flexing muscles, of sharpening pencils, of trying to put off the

evil day, and of just getting into the material. Much of that preliminary skirmishing stays in a manuscript even unto the second and third drafts. It is hard to cut because it is sometimes
hard to recognize one's own meanderings. But, once aware of
our own habits and the normal human fear of exposure, we can
overcome the tendency to go the long way around. In writing it
is not the shortest way home.

Although there are as many ways of writing as there are writers, one highly recommended and widely used technique is to
work in two distinct stages: (1) the first draft, which is written
with abandon – fully and freely and uncritically; (2) the second
draft, which is looked at by its author with a critical and analyt-
ical eye. Probably a few days, at least, should intervene between
these two stages, time enough to let the author change gears.

It seems to me that there are certain advantages in this way of
working. One is that the subconscious rises closer to the surface
if given a longer period of time to do so, rids us of inhibitions,
and does more of the work for us. Another is that early meanderings are more apparent and more easily overcome once an entire
first draft is complete, because there is a sense of the whole and
consequently a greater perspective. But I have known writers
who polish each paragraph as they go along and who apparently
work much better in shorter bursts. We can discover the method
that suits each of us best only by experimenting.

If the two-stage plan is followed, during the second stage
authors should be able to recognize how much stalling they are
actually doing. We all tend to play around the edges, trying not
to get our feet wet, when usually a dive into the deep part of the
pool is more effective. Jacques Barzun calls this timidity 'the
writer's insidious desire to put a cozy padded vest between his
tender self and that vague, hostile roaming animal known as the
audience.' His remedy is to 'convince yourself that you are
working in clay not marble, on paper not eternal bronze: let that
first sentence be as stupid as it wishes. No one will rush out and
print it as it stands.'[3]

It has been said that a play must be established in the first
thirty seconds. Although the techniques of the dramatist and the

author of expository prose are different, there is much to be
learned from the playwright – especially, in this context, the skill
of getting started. Dramatists, of course, have visual means to
help them: the set, living people, the costumes and props. But
they also use speech, and the first words that are chosen are of the
utmost importance. At the next play you see, think how much
information is given within the first few minutes. See how soon
it is made clear what the play is all about. We need go no further
than Shakespeare, as usual. *Romeo and Juliet* opens with:

> Two households, both alike in dignity,
> In fair Verona, where we lay our scene,
> From ancient grudge break to new mutiny,
> Where civil blood makes civil hands unclean.
> From forth the fatal loins of these two foes
> A pair of star-cross'd lovers take their life.

And Dylan Thomas began *Under Milk Wood* with his First Voice
saying very softly: 'To begin at the beginning.'[4] There is the
memorable first minute or so of *Our Town*, and, on a somewhat
different level, the shock opening of the mystery in which a
corpse falls out of the closet as soon as the curtain goes up. It is
clear from the start what these plays are going to be about.

I am not advocating shock openings for a scholarly work. But
a feel for this kind of thing will help an author discover how to
cut a lengthy preamble down to a few well-chosen words that
will give readers some sense of what they are in for. Here is a
good opening sentence for a scholarly work:

> On May 4, 1919, students in Peking demonstrated in protest against
> the Chinese government's humiliating policy toward Japan. There
> resulted a series of strikes and associated events amounting to a
> social ferment and an intellectual revolution. This rising tide was
> soon dubbed by the students the May Fourth Movement.[5]

The book is, not surprisingly, about the May Fourth Movement.
Erich Fromm began *The Sane Society* with: 'Nothing is more

common than the idea that we, the people living in the Western world of the twentieth century, are eminently sane.' We discover almost immediately that Fromm is going to challenge this idea when the second paragraph opens: 'Can we be so sure that we are not deceiving ourselves?'[6]

David Riesman started *The Lonely Crowd* without beating around the bush:

> This is a book about social character, and about the differences in social character between men of different regions, eras, and groups. It considers the ways in which different social character types, once they are formed at the knee of society, are then deployed in the work, play, politics, and child-rearing activities of society.[7]

If you feel that you are skirting around a subject or leading up to it on a long, winding path, think about what you actually want to say with this book after all the tortured months or perhaps years of research. Can you still see the forest for the trees? Try to sum up your book in a few words. Impossible? Not really. But even if you do not succeed, the mere attempt may help to get closer to the real subject and come to grips with it. Readers will be grateful.

Search, too, for repetitions. They are particularly rampant during the process of getting started. Circular prose should wind up in the circular file. A warm-up period is necessary in writing, as in most other activities, so the meanderings get down on paper. The trouble is that sometimes they stay there. Warming up should not be allowed to occupy valuable space in the finished product.

PART II

Length

The day of lengthy treatises of any sort may be passing. The luxury of spreading oneself in space or time simply does not fit in with modern technology. Verbosity is expensive. Books may necessarily become shorter and shorter except, of course, for best-sellers, which can still be allowed some width on the bookshelf because they pay their way. The time may come when the only fat books will be the wildly popular ones.

This trend would be sad if it were not true that shorter is often better. A long book is frequently long only because it has too many words. It is perhaps a commentary on present-day standards that we have to be driven to write with telling brevity not by the desire to communicate well but by the need to cut costs. Yet long before the age of soaring printing costs, the best writers whittled at their prose. Thoreau wrote in a letter to a friend: 'Don't suppose that you can tell it precisely the first dozen times you try, but at 'em again ... Not that the story need be long, but it will take a long time to make it short.'[8]

Cutting a manuscript is not simply a way of reducing length; it is also a way of strengthening communication. It is always hard to convince anyone that less is more, that the still small voice speaks louder, that fewer words are stronger, that a good thought needs no embellishment, and that one good sentence goes a long way. But there is a psychological reason for preferring brevity: 'By reducing the span of attention required we increase the force of the thought.'[9] Ideas come through more clearly if there are fewer of them in each sentence or paragraph. Sentences come through more clearly if there are fewer words in them, and one good word is worth two mediocre ones. With this standard in mind, pruning becomes a positive process, not merely cutting down or out, casting away, or bulldozing, but careful surgery that results in health, strength, and vitality.

There are two major ways of cutting a manuscript: one is by searching for repetitions and unneeded quotations and cutting out whole hunks; the other is to do what is known as 'inner cutting,' that is, eliminating paragraphs, sentences, and words. Strunk delivered the classic statement about pruning prose:

> Vigorous writing is concise. A sentence should contain no unnecessary words, a paragraph no unnecessary sentences, for the same

reason that a drawing should have no unnecessary lines and a machine no unnecessary parts. This requires not that the writer make all his sentences short, or that he avoid all detail and treat his subjects only in outline, but that every word tell.[10]

There used to be a schoolroom exercise called 'writing the précis.' I gather from contact with many students that such old-fashioned discipline is no longer inflicted on them. This is to be regretted, for working at a précis is as valuable to a writer as *barre* exercises are to a dancer. Making a précis consisted simply of summing up the essential points of a paragraph in one sentence, a hard, hateful task that required much thinking. But its benefits remain, and those who have undergone this kind of drill may be grateful for the training when they have to hack a path through a jungle of prose to let in a little sunlight. Writers who are trained by the précis will not often let their own prose ramble about.

Even after an author has eliminated from the manuscript all the vestiges of the thesis which may appear as unnecessary repetition, notices, tables, listings, digressions, and the paraphernalia that belong in the appendix or back matter, and has squeezed out all unnecessary verbiage, he or she may find that there is still more to cut. Sometimes there is material for several offshoot articles, and for authors who hate to waste anything, they can set this aside for future use and they need not feel that they have worked in vain.

Undigested Research

Many writers of theses think of their job as merely the presentation of research and the results therefrom. Writers of books must get beyond the mere public display of data: they must chew the material well, digest it, and turn it into something of their own. Some of the signs of still undigested research are too many tables and graphs, an over-abundance of notes, lengthy bibliographies, a rash of cross-references, and excessive listing.

In certain books, of course, tables are important and necessary. Books in some areas of social science can hardly get along without them, and they are creeping more and more into historical studies, as the computer spews out statistical information historians have never been able to tap before. But tables and graphs mixed in with the text are often merely a resurgence of the thesis. At best, a table or chart interrupts the flow of the manuscript, and if the interruption is allowed, there should be an excellent reason.

If a table is short, the facts may often be summed up and incorporated into the text. If the table is long and the information is truly more easily grasped in tabular form, it can perhaps be removed to an appendix.

When authors have put in months or, more probably, years on their research, it is hard for them to give up any of it. They use it all because it is at hand, just as some people climb mountains because they are there. That a table which is fruity with figures culled with indomitable patience from an out-of-the-way archive may be superfluous is not easy to accept. But this is a prime example of the shift in attitude from self to work necessary in transforming thesis to book. Authors have to forget how much time, sweat, grant money, and eye strain the table cost. Now they think only of the book and its readers.

The same considerations apply to notes. An excessively noted text is obviously not the way to the hearts and minds of most readers. One of the principal differences between a thesis and a book is that more documentation is needed in a thesis, for the examiner must judge the value of the candidate's sources and how well they have been used. But when a book is opened out from a thesis, readers assume that the author's sources are reliable, at least until they are given reason for doubt. The sources should now sink beneath the surface for the most part. They are still there if anyone should challenge a statement, but they don't need to be quite so evident. Reader interest has shifted from research to interpretation, from the statements of others to the author's own, from the mining of the ore to the metal itself.

When pondering the reduction of notes, it is well to consider which category each fits into: is it (a) a citation, (b) a comment,

(c) a cross-reference, or (d) an acknowledgment? The author should, of course, pin down direct quotations and acknowledge borrowings – comments are more difficult. Some notes fill in the picture and round out the text; some explain murky points that simply would take up too much room in the text; but others, although containing interesting information, are not absolutely vital. In general, explanatory notes are important, but those that raise side issues are not. The process of cutting, eliminating, and paring may well include as many cross-references as possible, for they annoy readers by requiring them to flip back and forth. Another reason to cut them out of the manuscript is the cost involved – and the possibility of errors in inserting the page numbers in page proof. If some cross-references must be used, it is well to make sure that 'see p. 14' is not just a casual remark but, if heeded, rewards readers for their effort in looking it up.

The following page, culled from no known book, may serve as illustration:

Victor Krasovsky, better known inside and outside Russia by his pen-name, Karel Kopek, was born in a Uighur family in Sverd-lovsk or somewhere in the Crimea in the year 1898.[1] Since Kopek's father was a premier danseur with the Bolshoi Ballet[2] and since we know that Kopek was brought up in Moscow,[3] we can consider him a Muscovite regardless of his place of birth. Kopek always thought of Moscow as his home; his fondness for this city is repeatedly expressed in his writings.[4]

Kopek's father was killed in 1900 when he crashed into the orchestra pit during a high leap.[5] The family, never very well off in any case, was now impoverished.[6] In 1909, at the age of 11, Kopek entered the Pavlovsk Elementary School on Bolotnaya Street.[7] At this school, he became friendly with a classmate, Nikolai Gorov-din, who was later to achieve great fame as an ornithologist,[8] and from whom we get an insight into Kopek's childhood and youth.[9] Kopek, moved no doubt by strong emotion, talks frankly of his school days in an article eulogizing Gorovdin at the time of his death. He said: 'For many years Gorovdin was my closest friend. We used to play hooky and go swimming in the Moskva together

– we played darts – stole sweets from the local store. We lounged around on street corners and watched the girls go by. Occasionally we studied.'[10]

Notes

1 There is some controversy about the date and place of Kopek's birth. Jonathan Larrabee in *Fifteen Hundred Modern Russian Short Stories* (Moscow, 1948), p. 84, mentions that Kopek was born in the Crimea in 1897. Arthur Field-Smythe in *A Short History of Russian Literature* (London, 1956) and the 'Note about the Author' at the end of Karel Kopek, *The Lazy Man's Donkey and Other Stories*, tr. Peter Twohig (New York, 1970), gives the date 1899 and the place Sverdlovsk. Phillip McGeoghan in *Modern Russian Fiction* (New Haven, 1971), p. 166, gives it as 1898 but provides no clue as to how he reached this date. I have calculated 1898 to be Kopek's year of birth from his article 'Russkoe Detstvo' in *Novaia Zhizn*, no. 1:23 (1959), in which he says that Gorovdin was a year younger than he. Gorovdin was born in 1899. Kopek also mentions that he left for Paris in 1924 when he was 26 years old. This also points to 1898 as his year of birth. Larrabee, Field-Smythe, and McGeoghan all agree that Kopek was born in the Crimea, but Heinegger in his chapter on early influences in *Der Symbolismus van Karel Kopek* states emphatically that he was born in Sverdlovsk and that his cradle is still there.
2 See Zbigniew Morovski, *The Evolution of a Russian Writer* (Prague, 1963).
3 Ibid., p. 24
4 The most famous of his descriptions of Moscow is found in 'A City at Dawn,' but almost all of his novels are laid in that city and are full of vivid descriptions of the streets and the people.
5 Morovski, p. 19
6 It is difficult to comprehend what 'impoverishment' means in this context. Kopek first studied with a private tutor and then went to school, and this can hardly be called a state of impov-

erishment, but he repeatedly emphasizes his childhood poverty and later financial difficulties; in 1935 at the age of 37, he said: 'I have been poor since childhood.'

7 I am indebted to Evgenii Narodny of Cochituate College for this information. Professor Narodny also attended the Pavlovsk School and remembers Kopek well, as a disagreeable individual given to spit balls and sarcastic remarks. Bolotnaya Street has since been renamed Marksistskaia.

8 Nikolai Gorovdin became a professor at Kiev University and received many honorary degrees in Eùrope and America. He is the author of *An Encyclopedia of Ornithology* and about fifty other books on the subject as well as many treatises and articles. He was also renowned as a chess player.

9 See Nikolai Gorovdin, *Some Memories of My Childhood*, tr. Laura Applegate (Boston, 1948).

10 Karel Kopek, 'Nikolai Gorovdin,' *Sovetskii Mir* (June, 1965)

In a book these notes can certainly be reduced; they are excessive even for a thesis. The factual information about Kopek's early life need not be noted since the reader will assume that the writer has done the research. The reader is quite willing to accept the date of birth the writer puts forward and is not anxious to get embroiled in a controversy about it. Again, the writer's method and means of coming to a decision are not now as important as the decision itself. The remarks about whether or not Kopek was poor fall into the same category. We don't really need to know much about Gorovdin for the purposes of this book, although it could be interesting sideline information. It might be well to keep note 9 because Gorovdin's book appears to be the sole source of information on Kopek's childhood and could conceivably round out the reader's knowledge of the subject. A reference for the direct quotation (note 10) is, as noted, mandatory in scholarly writing.

Sometimes lengthy bibliographies also have to be pared. A bibliography enables the reader to carry on further research and can be a helpful part of the book. But the reader now being served may or may not desire to go into the subject thoroughly.

In any event, this is not a list of all a candidate's research for the benefit of a committee of examiners; it is a list to help some readers find out more about the subject, and therefore need not include everything the author has read or everything that has ever been written on the subject.

The length and fullness of a bibliography in fact depend to a great extent upon the type of book. Whereas reduction of notes is nearly always advisable when turning a thesis into a book, bibliographies sometimes may not need trimming. Some bibliographies are pioneer work and are unavailable elsewhere; these obviously should be retained in their entirety. There are also varying degrees of selectivity in bibliographical material: some books are bibliographies in themselves. The author should look at the bibliography from the point of view of the reader, both the specialist and the general reader. What would specialists need to point them to further research, and what would general readers be likely to want? The shift here is, as in other matters, a shift in point of view. Just as an author anticipates in the index what the reader is apt to look for, so the author anticipates in the bibliography what the reader might want to pursue. There should always be enough information to dispel any mystery about where the book or document can be found.

One more sign of undigested research is excessive listing, the firstly, secondly, thirdly habit which is halfway between tabular form and text. Such listing may be more of the outline showing through. Some attempt should be made to weave the material into the text. At any rate, if *a*, *b*, and *c* are used, avoid what Theodore M. Bernstein, in *The Careful Writer*, calls a 'bastard enumeration.' That is, if the list starts out with (1) making an apple pie, the next item must not be (2) the manufacture of a blueberry pie. A listing of proposed steps in a diplomatic crisis which begins with (a) denunciation of commercial treaty, should not switch to (b) advising women and children to leave, and end (c) withdraw financial aid. It should read (a) denunciation of the commercial treaty, (b) advice to women and children to leave, and (c) withdrawal of financial aid. The entries should be grammatically parallel, whatever form is used. Elementary? Very difficult to remember, actually – and forever turning up wrong in scholarly manuscripts.

Another point to remember about listing is that when authors are launched on a firstly, secondly, thirdly sequence, they should deliver promptly on their promises. It is disconcerting to come across 'the third school of thought' when the first two schools are several paragraphs away. Even attentive readers tend to look back to make sure they and the author are counting right. A multi-paragraph listing is often necessary, but when this happens the announcement of *a, b, c* should not be in the paragraph that contains a full treatment of only the first item in the list. This is another elementary – and frequent – error.

Headings and sub-headings, too, are worth examining to see which should stay and which should not. Useful as they sometimes are, headings can also be the outline of the thesis showing through. Headings always have a textbook look. If the reader can be moved along without confusion simply by the text itself, headings should not be needed. But if a number of points of equal importance are being discussed, headings may make it easier to remember them, and give the reader a convenient reference.

Repetition

We all have a tendency to reiterate for emphasis – a self-defeating exercise because reiteration not only weakens the argument but obscures it. The effect is the same as that of using two adjectives where one will do. It seems as though two words ought to be twice as strong as one, but writing is not quantitative. Quality counts more than numbers.

Some authors use repetition deliberately to make sure their readers will not miss the point. But readers do not miss the implicit condescension. It is as if the author were saying: 'In case you missed this on the first round, here it is again. I didn't quite trust you to catch my meaning the first time.' We have again a crossover from the classroom technique of pampering the sleepy student.

Most repetition, however, is unintentional and could be eliminated. The author needs to step back and look at the work with
some perspective, to let the manuscript gather a little dust, and
then pick it up again. The repetition will then stand out.

One must beware particularly of repeating the same ideas in
different words. Authors will sometimes struggle to express their
meaning in one sentence, and then go on to the next where they
try a different combination of words to say the same thing instead of staying with the first sentence and making it clear.
Whenever writers come across 'in other words' at the beginning
of a sentence, they should pause and reflect. They may realize
that they are repeating by restatement. Probably most repetition
in manuscripts is a direct result of reluctance to revise one more
time. We plod on, slogging through the mud of our own prose
rather than taking the time to think of alternative routes and drier
paths. For most of us, thinking is always harder than acting.

Excessive Quoting

One of the first places to look for likely cuts in an overlong
manuscript is in the quoted material. Quotations enliven a page,
but when a book is peppered with them, they look like padding,
point to the author's unsureness, and become simply crutches
to lean upon. The reader begins to suspect that the author is letting others do the work. Instead of using a full quotation, an
author sometimes can achieve more by paraphrasing or perhaps
by quoting only a characteristic or striking word or phrase.
Before using a quotation, the author should ask: Does it make a
necessary point? Does it add concreteness? Does it explain what
he or she is talking about in fewer words?

We build upon one another's work. If we are struggling to
make a necessary point, and someone else has explained it better, we should be concerned only with giving the reader the best
possible break. Therefore, a quotation with (naturally) full credit
can be a means of clarification, a useful tool. The following quotation from H.W. Fowler should in this way make my point
clearer and reinforce what I am saying: 'A writer expresses him-

self in words that have been used before because they give his meaning better than he can give it himself, or because they are beautiful or witty, or because he expects them to touch a chord of association in his reader or because he wishes to show that he is learned or well read. Quotations due to the last motive are invariably ill advised.'[11]

Using a quotation because it is 'beautiful or witty' may also be ill advised, especially in a scholarly work. Beauty has its dangers, as has wit. The two qualities can delude us into thinking that a quotation is apt or useful in context, when it is not. I remember a book on politics whose writer had fallen in love with Finley Peter Dunne's creation, Mr Dooley, and couldn't resist quoting him. I love Mr Dooley too, but he almost ran away with that book. He was, in this case, a nuisance and a diversion. The author finally compromised by using two short excerpts that made a point, concretely, wittily, enjoyably, humanly – but not overwhelmingly.

The second reason I have given for quoting, to add concreteness, is of particular importance in scholarly writing. By using direct quotation, an author can keep the book from becoming overly abstract and give the reader, even the most academic, some relief from the empyreal world of the intellectual concept. In a well-chosen quotation we mentally hear the speaker's voice, and this silent echo adds an extra dimension to our understanding of the text. Such a direct quotation is always more forceful because the ideas have not been filtered through another person's mind.

In biography, of course, it is almost impossible to do without some of the subject's own words; at the least, omission of this made-to-order material would be a foolish waste. A stunning example of the skilful use of quotation is the following passage from Barbara Tuchman's *Stilwell and the American Experience in China*. Tuchman quoted General Stilwell in what she called 'one of the historic statements of the war.' He said: 'I claim we got a hell of a beating. We got run out of Burma and it is humiliating as hell.' The author added: 'The impact of the words was clean and hard. Stilwell's honesty cut through the pap and plush prose of Army public relations as the *San Francisco Chronicle* recalled at a later time, like a "sharp, salt wind."'[12]

There should be no need to point out that quoted matter should be accurate in every detail, but so many manuscripts are found faulty in this connection that it is worth reiterating. From an editorial point of view, the only changes that should be made in the quoted text are (1) an initial letter may be changed to a capital or a lower case letter; (2) a final punctuation mark may be changed to make the quotation fit into the syntax of the text. Otherwise, wording, spelling, capitalization, and the punctuation of the original must be kept intact. According to *The Chicago Manual of Style:*

> In a passage from a modern book, journal, or newspaper, an obvious typographical error may be silently corrected, but in a passage from an older work or from a manuscript source, any idiosyncrasy of spelling should generally be preserved, although in some cases the author may consider it desirable to modernize spelling and punctuation for the sake of clarity. The reader should be informed of any such alterations, either in a note or, in a book containing many such quotations, by an explanation in the preface or elsewhere.[13]

Some authors quote to such excess that they seem to be trying to save their readers a trip to the library. One young student thought he was doing the reader a service when, instead of giving a mere reference in a note, he provided great chunks of his sources word for word. This kind of generosity is bound to annoy readers who are quite capable of looking up references if they want to, unless, perhaps, the books are hidden away in a Tibetan monastery. With the advent of the Internet, lengthy quoting will be even less desirable: if sources are a mouse-click away, there is hardly any need to print excerpts. Then, perhaps, we shall see the day when the quotation as crutch will be virtually useless and scholars will be more inclined to manufacture their own beauty and wit, and all by themselves find the apt words to express their meaning.

Permissions

While we are on the subject of quotations, a word about permissions might be useful.

Permission to use a quotation in a thesis does not cover its use in a published work. A thesis writer may feel all that is necessary has been done if he or she has a friendly letter from Lord Pricklypear authorizing use of the family archives. The author and publisher may have a rude awakening when they discover that the generous earl's Aunt Agatha is suing for half a million dollars. Although most cases are not so shattering, books have been recalled from bookstores for just such reasons, and much money and sleep have been lost all around.

In the case of unpublished material (letters, for instance), it is also not enough to obtain permission from the library where such material has been deposited; permission must also be secured from the owner or from his or her estate. The writer of a letter (or his or her heirs or assigns) is the copyright owner. It is always best to track the copyright owner down, even if it takes time and patience, and get the owner, or his or her heir, to write another letter for your publisher's files giving you iron-clad permission. In the United Kingdom, however, a scholar is allowed (since 1956) to reproduce any unpublished manuscript or copy of one that is open to public inspection in a library or museum, beginning fifty years after the death of the author and one hundred years after creation of the work.

Usually it is not worthwhile to expend much effort to secure permission for the use of copyright material until the manuscript has been accepted by a publisher, since most publishers will not handle requests for permission unless the author furnishes the name of the house that will be issuing the book. In addition, the publisher will advise the author whether applications are required – in many cases, the application of the clause in the copyright law covering fair use or fair dealing makes requests unnecessary, but publishers differ in their views about it. As well, the publisher may have stipulations to make about market rights which should be incorporated in permission requests. Needless to say, because of the extra trouble involved, the inclusion of a large number of long quotations from copyright works does not add to the attractiveness of a manuscript in the eyes of a prospective publisher.

It would also be unwise to begin to transform a thesis on a modern author into a book in which there is extensive quoting from the author's works, without first enquiring from the author's publisher or agent whether permission is likely to be given. Such an enquiry has the added value of just possibly interesting the original publisher in the study, or of producing a warning that someone else has pre-empted the topic.

PART III

Once the signs of a thesis have been eliminated, the author should have a manuscript that he or she can begin to work with and shape into a book. The first step in this more positive process is to decide how much background information the new readers will need. This is rarely easy, for readers' knowledge will vary from subject to subject and also from time to time. High school students of today, for example, are far more knowledgeable in certain areas (particularly scientific ones) than their counterparts of some years ago. There is a well-known maxim that can be adapted to these circumstances: never underestimate the intelligence of a reader, or overestimate his or her knowledge.

To create a self-contained book authors have to try to put themselves in the reader's skin. They must perform an act of imagination and of perception that is not required of thesis writers. A scholar engrossed in a specialty does not find it easy to think beyond it to communicate with others who do not have the same knowledge. Even in everyday communication, we tend to assume either that a person has no need of explanation or that our subject must be explained to death. Those who learn to fill others' gaps without condescension, offering just as much as the others want to know, but no more, develop a skill that is as useful in everyday life as it is on the printed page. It is particularly useful, of course, for a teacher. It is related to the ability to listen selectively.

Every book has a context which can enrich and deepen its meaning and add to its interest. The fragmentary piece of life captured in print is never the whole story. And although focus is essential, paradoxically a book is made more self-contained by enlarging its horizons. When Harvey Cox began *The Feast of Fools* with an 'Overture' in which he gave the history of the medieval Feast of Fools, he said: 'This is not a historical treatise and I recall the Feast of Fools only as a symbol of the subject of this book.'[14] But it *is* important background material for an understanding of his theme. Garrett Mattingly gave his readers an entire panorama of Europe in the fifteenth century in four pages in *Catherine of Aragon*, a fine piece of background writing, imparting a feeling of the times without too many bewildering figures and events.[15] Margaret Mead's sweeping introduction to *Culture and Commitment* placed her theme in the wide context of twentieth-century culture:

> An essential and extraordinary aspect of man's present state is that, at this moment in which we are approaching a world-wide culture and the possibility of becoming fully aware citizens of the world in the late twentieth century, we have simultaneously available to us for the first time examples of the ways men have lived at every period over the last fifty thousand years ... At the time that a New Guinea native looks at a pile of yams and pronounces them 'a lot' because he cannot count them, teams at Cape Kennedy calculate the precise second when an Apollo mission must change its course if it is to orbit around the moon. This is a situation that has never occurred before in human history.[16]

With this preparation we are ready for the author's first chapter, which begins: 'The distinctions I am making among three different kinds of culture ... are a reflection of the period in which we live.'[17] Since Mead has already given us a ten-page review of the period in which we live, what she says in the course of the book is readily understood.

In deciding what kind of background will prepare the thesis for its opening out into a book, a young scholar might find it helpful to read a number of introductions to scholarly books in other fields. Friends who have no knowledge whatsoever of the field also may be able to provide valuable advice, if they read the opening chapter and specify what kind of information they need to understand it.

After an author has decided how much and what kind of background material to present, there remains the question of where to put it. A large lump of background usually stalls the forward movement of a manuscript; therefore, if much background must be given all at once, it is best to put it near the beginning. The most difficult but the most effective way to provide the reader with background information is to give it in small quantities at a time and as needed.

Some background can be introduced by simply explaining briefly when an unknown name or term crops up. In the following quotation from a book about Rabindranath Tagore, the author weaves in his background skilfully (250 pages along in the text):

> The opening decades of the twentieth century brought major political changes to the Hindu-British relationship in Bengal, and therefore to Tagore's position in his own province. The spread of English education and consequently of English political ideals had by 1900 produced a large and vocal school of moderate nationalists. The British bureaucracy, led by the conservative Lord Curzon from 1898 to 1905, looked down on this Anglicized class as a deracinated minority, and grievously affronted it by partitioning Bengal in 1905 into Hindu and Muslim majority areas. The ensuing anti-British agitation ... produced a new extremist school of nationalists who rejected both British rule and British influence on Indian culture. Tagore parted company with the extremists, and was regarded by them as a defector.[18]

The ins and outs of Hindu–British relationships in Bengal are not known to most of us, and at this point in the narrative even specialists may need a reminder of the climate in which Tagore worked. But the author has not left Tagore on the sidelines while interjecting a little British and Indian history. He has kept him close by and pulled him back into the paragraph, keeping us aware that Tagore is the central figure moving against the historical landscape. This background does not slow down the text but deepens and enhances it.

Such background, of course, may have been provided in the thesis, but the new readers of the book probably need a fuller briefing than the doctoral committee. Authors who give them the right amount in the right place will have taken a long step toward involving their audience and creating a self-contained book.

Clarity

Clarity is an editor's touchstone, an author's goal. There is no communication without it, and so it becomes an absolute first in any consideration of style. Often the impediment to clarity is not inability to express a thought so much as inability to think clearly. Much bad writing comes from the belief that writing and thinking are disparate activities. Although it is possible that a person can think well but not be able to write well, and that writing can seem facile and clear even if there is not much thought behind it, the best writing is usually an ideal marriage of thought and word. Obscurity can be the result of a brain working so fast that words come out in a bewildering ava- lanche, but confused sentences are far more likely to be the result of muddle-headedness. It is more pleasant, of course, to believe that one's brain is working too fast than that it is mud- dled. Ambrose Bierce said, 'Good writing ... is clear thinking made visible.'[19] 'Let the meaning choose the word, and not the other way about,' was George Orwell's sound advice.[20]

The teaching of English as grammar has implanted the wrong order in our minds. The average teacher of English 'appears to attempt to place the emphasis upon writing rather than writing- about-something-for-someone.'[21] As a result we tend to think first of words (this is where all the high-sounding pomposity comes from) rather than meanings. We become overawed by mere symbols when we should be paying attention to realities.

Thinking is not always a verbal type of cerebration. There is some evidence that the wordless half of the brain could help us in getting words on paper if we would only let it. Perhaps a lively liaison between the two halves of the brain is indeed the source of great writing. Orwell's advice to put off using words as long as possible and first to 'get one's meaning as clear as one can through pictures or sensations'[22] seems to bear this out, and we know that Einstein used both halves with superlative ease:

> When Einstein was asked how he arrived at some of his most original ideas, he explained the he rarely thought in words at all. 'A thought comes, and I may try to express it in words afterwards,' he said. His concepts first appeared through 'physical entities' – certain signs and more or less clear images that he could reproduce and combine. These elements were 'of visual and some of muscular type,' he added. 'Conventional words or other signs have to be sought for laboriously only in a secondary stage, when the mentioned associative play is sufficiently established and can be reproduced at will.'[23]

However the author's own mind works, it is he or she who stands between the reader and confusion. I once wrote on the margin of a manuscript: 'This paragraph is very confusing.' The author replied: 'But the situation was confused.' My reply was: 'Keep your head when all about you are losing theirs.'

The way to achieve clarity, therefore, is to be precise, first in thought, then in expression. Truth of expression corresponds to scholarly truth: exactness of language comes from honesty, patient searching, and a refusal to settle for second best. This kind of truth should be as important to scholars as the exactness of their thoughts. There is 'a lie of the approximate word,' as Grace Paley puts it, as well as a lie of 'the brilliant sentence you love the most.'[24] Morris Philipson, director of the University of Chicago Press, has commented: 'The most significant purpose of language [is] communication between people – or, ideally, communion among people ... What is execrable is what misleads, what traduces, what injects error, what cloaks the absence of thought or feeling, what pretends to be something other than it is, what is false.'[25] A person whose words and deeds match is said to have integrity, or wholeness. A person's writing has integrity when words and thoughts match.

Abstractions

In seeking clarity, the scholarly writer faces the major problem of trying to present abstract ideas to the reader. Human nature tends to reject the vague and the general in favour of the specific and the concrete. Consequently, the writer must somehow bring abstractions down to earth.

The problem in dealing clearly with abstract ideas occurs because thinking comes before words. As George Orwell explained it: 'When you think of a concrete object, you think wordlessly and then, if you want to describe the thing you have been visualizing you probably hunt about till you find the exact words that seem to fit it. When you think of something abstract you are more inclined to use words from the start, and unless you make a conscious effort to prevent it, the existing dialect will come rushing in and do the job for you, at the expense of blurring or even changing your meaning.'[26]

This 'existing dialect' is the enemy; its use leads to pale, dull, cliché-ridden, and incomprehensible prose. It leads away from rather than toward communication.

William Howells in *Back of History* handled the abstract word 'culture' by using homely detail. He ended one paragraph, 'Culture is all those things that are *not* inherited biologically,' and began the next: 'Instead, culture consists of everything that has ever been accepted as a way of doing or thinking, and so taught by one person to another.' But he was still speaking in general terms; so, after an explanation of teaching and learning, he narrowed down: 'Let us take some simple examples from what would be a very simple culture. A digging stick of a particular kind, for digging up wild vegetables for food, is culture. So is using a skin for keeping warm. So is the idea of appointing a war chief for the group, or the idea of marriage.'[27]

When writing about abstract ideas, we tend to classify rather than describe. A good point to remember is that scientific language classifies; and all writers are affected by the popularity of science and the vogue for using scientific terms. But there is more reality in a blade of grass than in the concept of chlorophyll. We may learn how to categorize fish but forget how a fresh-caught mackerel tastes. We may know the names of birds, families, and species, but be deaf to their songs. So the addiction to the scientific term has its dangers, and one of them is a deadening effect upon writing and speaking. The more technical we get, the more we use the interchangeable, standardized parts of technical language, and neglect concrete, sensual description.

The writer of the following has been more than ordinarily affected by 'scientism,' as Wilson Follett calls this kind of language: 'This aspect was, of course, more significant in terms of personalized, individual relationships. Another aspect of relations, not less affected by personal factors was dealt with, however, as an institutional problem.'[28]

Contrast that uncertain paragraph with this one, whose author described rather than classified, worked from the particular to the general, and gave first the evidence of the senses:

It is interesting to contemplate a tangled bank, clothed with many plants of many kinds, with birds singing on the bushes, with various insects flitting about, and with worms crawling through the damp earth, and to reflect that these elaborately constructed forms, so different from each other, and dependent upon each other in so complex a manner, have all been produced by laws acting upon us. These laws taken in the largest sense, being Growth with Reproduction; Inheritance ... Variability ... Ratio of Increase so high as to lead to a Struggle for Life ... Natural Selection ... Divergence of Character and the Extinction of less-improved forms.[29]

This is an excerpt from the final paragraph of Darwin's *Origin of*

Species – a book that seems to have communicated its message to the world.

John Dewey, in his essay 'The Influence of Darwinism on Philosophy,' told some of that story:

> The conceptions that had reigned in the philosophy of nature and knowledge for two thousand years, the conceptions that had become the familiar furniture of the mind, rested on the assumption of the superiority of the fixed and final ... In laying hands upon the sacred ark of absolute permanency ... the 'Origin of Species' introduced a mode of thinking that ... was bound to transform the logic of knowledge.[30]

Dewey himself pinned down the general by using particular terms: 'familiar furniture of the mind' and 'sacred ark of absolute permanency.'

Using metaphor or analogy, as in the above passages, is one way of making abstractions more understandable. Introducing people into the text is another. Alfred North Whitehead, in discussing the conflict between religion and science, told how early theologians 'deduced from the Bible opinions concerning the nature of the physical universe.' He not only gave a specific illustration of this statement but introduced a character:

> In the year A.D. 535, a monk named Cosmas wrote a book which he entitled *Christian Topography*. He was a travelled man who had visited India and Ethiopia; and finally he lived in a monastery at Alexandria, which was then a great centre of culture. In this book, basing himself upon the direct meaning of Biblical texts as construed by him in a literal fashion, he denied the existence of the antipodes, and asserted that the world is a flat parallelogram whose length is double its breadth.[31]

Here is not only an idea but the man who held the idea; the idea becomes more memorable because we know something about the man.

'Good writing,' according to John K. Galbraith, 'and this is especially important in a subject such as economics, must also involve the reader in the matter at hand. It is not enough to explain. The images that are in the mind of the writer must be made to reappear in the mind of the reader, and it is the absence of this ability that causes much economic writing to be condemned, quite properly, as abstract.'[32]

Totalitarian jargon (whether communist or fascist) is a conspicuous modern phenomenon that can smother the thoughts of scholars as well as adherents in the grey dust of easy abstractions. 'Collectivization,' 'cadres,' 'rectification,' and that horror, 'co-operativization,' are all examples of words of category rather than of description. These heavy nouns are, according to Barzun, 'static and inclusive' phrases:

> ... they deny the doer and replace him by an activity, a process (a favorite word) which is therefore unchanging, eternal, and which gives the user the sense of being 'scientific' through 'covering' the events by abstraction ... This sort of writing, easy to write and dull to read, is the surest protection against the critical analysis of thought. It sounds as if its meaning were not only lucid but important, for example: 'This is undertaken in the context of comprehensive patient care and includes theory and supervised practice related to the assumption of a leadership role.' Who is doing what? No one; nothing. This part of a nurse's training has been lifted from the world of bedpans and wrinkled sheets to the abode where the eternal abstractions are.[33]

What happens ultimately when a concept is left in the 'abode of eternal abstractions' and not brought down to earth where the human mind can understand it is grimly illustrated in the explanation given by Lieutenant William Calley, during his trial for killing civilians at My Lai: 'When my troops were getting massacred and mauled by an enemy I couldn't see, I couldn't feel and I couldn't touch,' he explained, 'nobody in the military ever described them as anything other than Communism ... They didn't give it a race, they didn't give it a sex, they didn't give it an age. They never let me believe it was just a philosophy in a man's mind. That was my enemy out there.'[34]

Abstract words, when they move too far away from humanity and reality, can even kill.

Pace and Build

Pace, or rhythm, is another factor in good writing. Pace helps to produce the forward movement necessary to hold the reader's interest and to avoid 'the slow, pedantic crawl of scholarly prose,' in Edwin O. Reischauer's phrase.

The analogy of the drama is helpful. Pace is an exceedingly important ingredient in the production of any play and to set it is a part of a director's job. Comedy is played at a fast pace; tragedy is slower. But whatever the pace is, it is not accidental.

Although the reader may not be aware of this quality in a straightforward piece of expository writing, it exists, and it is established by the author. The passages that lag, the ones that are redundant, the words that slow down and impede the flow of thought, diminish the pace and make a piece of writing static and lifeless.

The elimination of unnecessary words is one way to achieve forward movement. The use of active verbs is another. The third step is a matter of ear, of listening to one's own words – reading aloud perhaps, but in any case listening. A perfectly clear and perfectly grammatical sentence can still grate on the ear. We all have prose rhythms that we prefer, not only through habit, but no doubt by character and temperament. And since writing is individual or nothing, we tend to use these rhythms as we write. This inner rhythm is a vital ingredient of style. We learn a lot about ourselves when we discover what kind of pace we prefer. P.G. Wodehouse darts at a fast bicycle clip; Winston Churchill rolls like a ship; E.B. White strolls but never meanders from the path.

Pace is strongly affected by word order. A simple change in the order of words can not only alter the meaning of a sentence completely but speed it up or slow it down. On a grander scale, the organization of the manuscript as a whole affects the pace. The old Aristotelian beginning, middle, and end construction is still valid, and the magic number three (the three acts of a play, for instance) in some mysterious way satisfies a deep psychological instinct and works well.

Beginnings and endings require watching and working over. The first and last words of sentences, the first and last sentences of paragraphs, the first and last paragraphs of chapters, the first and last chapters of a manuscript, linger longest in the reader's mind and should be the strongest points. Nothing should waver at the beginning or peter out at the end. The last half of the last sentence of the concluding chapter of *Origin of Species* reads: '... whilst this planet has gone cycling on according to the fixed law of gravity, from so simple a beginning endless forms most beautiful and most wonderful have been, and are being evolved.'[35] How much less effective this last sentence would have been if Darwin had written: 'Endless forms ... are being evolved whilst this planet has gone cycling on according to the fixed law of gravity.' It cannot be accidental that he ended with the theme of evolution.

In organizing the pace and structure of a book, a sense of story is often helpful. William Howells said that he 'tried to make a single story of the human background' in *Back of History*.[36] Many a manuscript has been unsnarled by giving it a simple chronological sequence that is actually a kind of story line. For any sequence of ideas, development of an argument, or pursuit of research, there is a natural structure which, once found, enables a reader to follow more easily and with greater interest than if the facts are merely strung one after the other like beads. There is still in all of us an atavistic memory of the technique of the story told around the campfire.

Readers will continue to follow if they feel they are going somewhere, deepening their insight, satisfying their curiosity, or extending their knowledge, but if they have to stand still or go in circles, they may become bored. 'Build,' a technical term used in the drama to describe the way in which a scene or a play builds up to a climax, thus can also be applied to the forward movement within a manuscript – as a whole, by chapter, or in the smaller units of sentence and paragraph.

Authors and Editors

When an author turns a thesis into a book, he or she is often working with an editor for the first time, and is not quite sure what to expect. The editor will probably turn out to be a person who, oddly enough, is just as interested as the author is in producing a good book and who stands ready with a blue pencil to unravel tangled sentences, see to it that commas and capitals are in the right places, pick up loose ends, weed the unwanted words, passive verbs, and infelicitous metaphors, and get across the idea that even if things are not quite right, they can be fixed.

It may sometimes seem to an author that an editor takes an occupational delight in finding flaws. Yet the editor would be of little use if he or she did not scrutinize the manuscript and occasionally suggest the removal of a crenellated turret here and there from the author's dream castle, or the addition of a stronger arch. Nevertheless the author remains in full control of his or her own work. It is the author's privilege to reject editorial advice, although it may be foolish to do so. If the author has doubts whether a particular word should be used, or a particular sentence recast, or a section cut out, then the author should find out exactly why the editor recommends such a move. It is up to the editor to explain satisfactorily, and the author should present his or her own point of view if it differs. This kind of dialogue is necessary, not for the peace of mind of either author or editor, but for the sake of the book. An editor does not and cannot be expected to have the same grasp of subject matter as the author, and the author may not have the same grasp of print or understanding of the reader's needs. Therefore, many points often have to be threshed out. But the final decision belongs, as a matter of course, to the author.

A good editor will also give an author confidence in his or her own powers. Research and writing are lonely occupations. It is easy to become discouraged in solitary confinement. The mere human contact with another mind, particularly one that is not competitive but is as eager as the author to make the jumble into a good book, can be encouraging. Most editors are careful of an author's feelings and alert to his or her good points. They can often give hope that there is a way out of the morass. They have doubtless seen far worse manuscripts and their range of experience, like doctors' (which gives a patient confidence simply because they have seen everything), can make an author feel that his or her book is not a candidate for the worst book of the year, but indeed a pretty good one that can be made better, can perhaps even be made into a fine one. This psychological lift can be an important ingredient in the making of a book.

Creating anything is like holding a bird in the hand. Hold it too tightly and it will be hurt and never fly; hold it too loosely and it will escape too soon. An editor's job is to show authors how to clasp and unclasp that hand, so their ideas may fly on strong wings.

NOTES

1   William Strunk, Jr, and E.B. White, *The Elements of Style*, 2nd ed. (New York: Macmillan, 1972), xii.
2   Frederick C. Crews, *The Pooh Perplex: A Freshman Casebook* (New York: Dutton, 1963).
3   Jacques Barzun, *On Writing, Editing, and Publishing* (Chicago: University of Chicago Press, 1971), 8, 9.
4   Dylan Thomas, *Under Milk Wood: A Play for Voices* (New York: James Laughlin, 1954).
5   Chow Tse-tsung, *The May Fourth Movement* (Cambridge: Harvard University Press, 1960).
6   Erich Fromm, *The Sane Society* (New York: Holt, Rinehart and Winston, 1955).
7   David Riesman, *The Lonely Crowd: A Study of the Changing American Character* (New Haven: Yale University Press, 1950).
8   Henry David Thoreau, *Walden and Other Writings*, introd. by Joseph Wood Krutch (New York: Bantam Books, 1962), 21.

9 Wilson Follett, *Modern American Usage: A Guide* (New York: Hill & Wang, 1966), 14.

10 Strunk and White, *The Elements of Style*, 69.

11 H.W. Fowler, *A Dictionary of Modern English Usage*, 2nd ed., rev. by Sir Ernest Gowers (New York: Oxford University Press, 1965), s.v. 'Quotation.'

12 Barbara Tuchman, *Stilwell and the American Experience in China, 1911–1945* (New York: Macmillan, 1970), 300.

13 *The Chicago Manual of Style*, 14th ed. rev. (Chicago: University of Chicago Press, 1993), 358.

14 Harvey Cox, *The Feast of Fools* (Cambridge: Harvard University Press, 1969).

15 Garrett Mattingly, *Catherine of Aragon* (Boston: Little, Brown & Co., 1941), 3–7.

16 Margaret Mead, *Culture and Commitment: A Study of the Generation Gap* (Garden City, NY: Doubleday, 1970), xv.

17 Ibid., 1.

18 Stephen N. Hay, *Asian Ideas of East and West: Tagore and His Critics in Japan, China, and India* (Cambridge: Harvard University Press, 1970).

19 Ambrose Bierce, *Write It Right: A Little Blacklist of Literary Faults* (New York and Washington: Meale Publishing Co., 1909), 5.

20 George Orwell, 'Politics and the English Language,' in *Shooting an Elephant and Other Essays* (London: Secker and Warburg, 1950), 100.

21 Wendell Johnson, 'You Can't Write Writing,' in *The Use and Misuse of Language*, ed. S.I. Hayakawa (Greenwich, CT: Fawcett Publications, Inc., 1962), 103.

22 Orwell, 'Politics and the English Language,' 99, 100.

23 Maya Pines, 'We Are Left-Brained or Right-Brained,' *New York Times Magazine*, 9 September 1973.

24 Grace Paley, 'Some Notes on Teaching: Probably Spoken,' in *Writers As Teachers: Teachers As Writers*, ed. Jonathan Baumbach (New York: Holt, Rinehart and Winston, 1970), 205.

25 Morris Philipson, Foreword, *On Writing, Editing, and Publishing*, by Jacques Barzun (Chicago: University of Chicago Press, 1971).

26 Orwell, 'Politics and the English Language,' 100.

27 William Howells, *Back of History: The Story of Our Own Origins* (Garden City, NY: Doubleday, 1954), 46.

28 Follett, *Modern American Usage*, s.v. 'Scientism.'
29 Charles Darwin, *Origin of Species* (New York: D. Appleton & Co., 1860), 423–4.
30 John Dewey, *The Influence of Darwinism on Philosophy and Other Essays* (New York: Henry Holt & Co., Inc., 1910), 1.
31 Alfred North Whitehead, *Science and the Modern World* (New York: Macmillan, 1925), 163.
32 John K. Galbraith, 'The Language of Economics,' in *Economics, Peace, and Laughter* (Boston: Houghton Mifflin, 1971), 29.
33 Jacques Barzun, 'The Language of Learning and Pedantry,' in *The House of Intellect* (New York: Harper & Brothers, 1959), 233.
34 *New York Times*, 23 February 1971.
35 Darwin, *Origin of Species*, 416, 424.
36 Howells, *Back of History*, 361.

chapter six

An Academic Author's Checklist

BARBARA B. REITT

After fifteen years of editing scholarly books, first as a university press staff member and then as a freelancer, I returned to school to study the history of book publishing. Once back into the academic routine, I was confronted with the need to acquire teaching experience. To my joy – and lasting edification, for the teacher learns so much more than the student – my department gave me the opportunity to develop and teach a seminar on writing for graduate students.[1] The course proved to be quite popular, and I began to get requests to present its 'essence' in a one-day workshop for junior faculty as well as students. At first I refused, doubting that enough of the essential content could be covered in so short a time. But the assistant dean was persistent and I relented.

My problem was to find a way to present participants in one-day sessions with the same ideas the students of the longer course were exploring. A definition of good scholarly and scientific writing was not a topic we could probe deeply in one day, but it was hardly a topic we could ignore. The checklist that follows was my solution. In it I attempted to capture the essential elements that students and I debated in the quarter-long courses. It presents the kinds of questions that a scholar or scientist must ask of any completed work – questions, therefore, the scholarly editor or referee must also consider. It may be that 'checklist' is a misnomer, for I never intended that the questions be treated as discrete items, answered one by one and in the same order. Rather, many items imply a number of the others, or cannot be answered fully until others are answered too. Moreover, no one report or monograph contains material that relates to all the questions here posed. Despite such limitations, a list of reminders like this one can be helpful. It serves to get mental wheels turning, stimulating a writer, a referee, or an editor to probe issues that might otherwise be overlooked or forgotten.

The list has been changed often, and should continue to be changed. Anyone caring to use it can do so productively *only* by changing it, personalizing it, making it useful for whatever task is at hand. The version that follows is an update, more than twenty years later, of the version I handed out in workshops. The changes reflect additional years of editing, the appearance of new resources for academic editors, and – to some extent – the effect of the electronic revolution on publishing.[2]

AN ACADEMIC AUTHOR'S CHECKLIST

Purpose and organization of the checklist

Intended for academic and scientific writers in all fields, this checklist describes a level of performance that is both idealistic and practical. It can be used by authors who wish to assess their own early drafts as objectively as possible; it can also be used by readers other than the author as a guide for criticizing a colleague's work, providing a means for identifying its weak and strong points. The checklist assists the critical reader, whether the author or not, to objectify the material being evaluated and to isolate important elements of academic and scientific written work so that it can be judged as journal editors and readers would judge it.

The checklist is organized so that the most important and profound questions are posed earlier. The final section lists tasks that are normally not completed until a final draft is being prepared. Of course, not all points listed under each section are relevant to each and every report or book a scholar or scientist might write; every scholarly or scientific work, however, must be (and, in fact, will be) judged for its completeness, authority, expertness, singularity, and finesse.

Is the draft, as it is written, complete?

What is the problem (question, issue) that the work sets out to solve?
Does it achieve a solution (resolution)?
If a full solution is not reached, why not?
- Is a complete solution not possible? Not possible at present?
- Is the evidence incomplete? Faulty? Inappropriate?
- Is the logic of presentation faulty?
- Is the methodology flawed?
- Does the problem need recasting?
Is the solution reached the best one among the possible answers?
Is the presentation of the material fully logical and coherent?
- Are there gaps readers must fill in for themselves?
- Are there loose ends that suggest alternative lines of thought?
- Are all steps explicit and in the right order?
- Are basic premises or assumptions acknowledged?
Is any information in the draft unnecessary?
- Do illustrative materials amplify or only repeat information in the text?
- If corollary materials are included, do they contribute to the main point or have a clear use for readers?
- Are two bits of information offered when one will do?
- Is there too much background or introductory material?
Is the significance of the solution apparent to the reader?
- Is the problem, to begin with, worth solving?
- What further research or study is implied by the work's completion?
- What uses can the work have?

Is the work, as it is written, authoritative?

Is the solution (information, hypothesis) presented based on an appropriate mixture of the writer's and others' work?
- Is the use of others' work excessive?
- Is the reliance on derived authority excessive? Are quotations and references carrying the weight of the argument?
- Have important authorities in the subject been ignored?

Is the solution based on an appropriate mix of primary and secondary sources?

Does the writer give evidence of wearing disciplinary blinders?
- Are relevant sources and experts from related fields overlooked?
- Have contiguous subject areas been explored for possibly valuable evidence or resources?

Are all the sources cited genuinely relevant and necessary?
- Do all sources contribute to the solution in a positive manner?
- Is a combative or adversarial stance taken for merely rhetorical reasons? Or is the argument, implicit or explicit, a genuine one?

Is the balance between published and unpublished sources justifiable?

If most of the sources are unpublished,
- have they been subjected to any review?
- are they up-to-date?
- have they been disproven in the literature?
- have they been discarded by their authors?
- should they have been replaced by published sources?
- have their authors given explicit permission for their use in a published work?

If most of the sources are published,
- are they the best sources that could be used?
- should any be replaced by unpublished sources?
- is 'fair use' (or 'fair dealing') being made of them, or is formal permission to use them necessary?[3]

Are all acknowledgments of indebtedness made? Has permission to acknowledge personal assistance been obtained?

Is the work, as it is written, expert?

Is the solution based on evidence, and is the evidence unambiguously and fully described?

Is the solution (resolution, conclusion, hypothesis) the result of the correct use of appropriate methodology?
- Is the method chosen the right one for this problem?
- Is the method employed correctly, that is, are the methodological procedures sound?

If the method used is a traditional one,
- is it used correctly?
- have any changes been made in parts of the method? Correctly? Justifiably?
- is it the best method to use for this problem?

If the method used is one that has been abandoned or gone unused for a long time,
- are the reasons for returning to it now clear to readers?
- are the reasons sound ones?

If the method used is a new one,
- is it original or borrowed from a colleague's unpublished work?
- does the method itself need explanation or justification?
- is the reason for not using a traditional or established method clear? Is the use of a new, perhaps unique, method more than just *justifiable* – is it *justified*?
- which is the real purpose of the work, to present the new method or to solve the ostensible problem? If both, is the existence of a dual purpose acknowledged and handled clearly?

Is the description of method clear enough that another person could replicate it?

Is the work, as it is written, singular?

Does it provide new information or hypotheses, or does it contribute corroborative evidence to an existing body of knowledge?

Which elements, exactly, in the work are unique, original, completely new? Are they highlighted appropriately?

Which elements, though not new to this field or specialty, are new to other groups of readers who have been overlooked before? Might such groups include:
- foreign readers?
- readers with regional interests?
- readers with national interests?
- generalists?
- interdisciplinary specialists?
- specialists in an allied field?
- novices?
- students? At what level or levels?
- theoreticians?
- clinicians? Readers in various applied sciences, disciplines?

Is the work directed carefully and appropriately to a specific group of readers?

What kind of information does the draft provide its readers? What mixture of new and established information?

Is the information timely or timeless?

How specialized is the information?

Who needs the information? For what purpose(s)?

Is the same information already available to readers?
- To which readers?
- Where?
- Is it widely or readily available?
- Is it more expensively or more cheaply available already?
- Is it as up to date?
- Is this work, in short, an improved source of existing information?

Is the work a fully refined written product – is it finished?

These questions should be answered last, when a final draft is being prepared. The answers will vary, depending on the preferences of individual editors or publishing houses. Journals and book publishers often publish instructions for authors, covering

many of the points touched on here. Lacking such specific guidance from a prospective publisher, an author can follow the
models provided by the publisher in the form of current issues
of a journal or recently published books. Further details are
readily available in style manuals published for specific subject
areas, many of them emanating from the same societies that
publish the journals and books.[4]

In answering the questions in this section, a writer, referee, or
editor is not evaluating the scientific soundness or the scholarship of a piece so much as extending an important courtesy to a
publishing staff. A report or monograph that is genuinely finished is easier and less expensive to publish quickly and well. It
may therefore also have a better chance of being published.

Is the title an accurate description of the contents?
- Is its word order useful to indexers and researchers?
- Does it contain the best key words?
- Can it be misunderstood?
- Is it a cliché?

Are key words, if requested, well chosen and complete?

Is the abstract, if required for an article, an accurate description
of the work?
- Is it the correct length?
- Is it in the correct form (i.e., narrative or structured)?

Does the draft contain any unnecessary elements?
- Can any words, phrases, sentences, paragraphs, or sections
  be deleted?
- Can the opening be deleted or shortened?
- Can the closing be deleted or shortened?

Is the sentence structure sound and varied?
- Do all the subjects agree with their verbs?
- Do the main clauses contain the most important points; the
  dependent clauses, the subsidiary ones?
- Does the active voice prevail?
- Is the action expressed by the verbs, not by stacked-up
  nouns and phrases? (For example: 'Administrators welcomed the program's new cost effectiveness' and not 'The
  newly established cost effectiveness of the program was an
  innovation much welcomed by the administration.')

- Are sentence lengths varied? Is there a mixture of rhetorical types?

Are spelling, word compounding, capitalization, and the use of figures and abbreviations consistent?

Is all quoted material perfectly correct? Double-checked?

Is the vocabulary non-racist and non-sexist?[5]

Are all errors of grammar and usage searched out and corrected?

Are tables and illustrations finished and ready for production?[6]
- Can any be deleted (they should amplify, not repeat, text)?
- Are they properly captioned? Properly numbered (no inserts)?
- Are they clearly labelled and keyed to the text?
- Are all totals and percentages double-checked for accuracy?

The covering letter

Is the covering letter brief?

Does it include:
- the work's full title?
- the main author's full name, mailing address, business telephone number, and e-mail address?
- institutional affiliations of all the authors?

Does it describe the work, not by summarizing its contents, but by noting its contribution to the field and its relevance to this journal's contents or to this publisher's backlist and market?

Does it offer only the biographical information about the author that indicates his or her qualifications for doing the research or reasons for writing the article?

NOTES

1 See 'The Editor Turns Teacher,' *Scholarly Publishing* 2, no. 3 (April 1980): 56–66.
2 The teacher has turned back to editing full-time, occasionally teaching short courses. For the original checklist, see 'The Academic Author's Checklist,' *Scholarly Publishing* 16, no. 1 (Oct. 1984): 65–72.

3 In this editor's experience, too few academic authors understand
   even the basics of copyright law, much less the finer points having to
   do with fair use (also known as fair dealing). The impact of the electronic revolution and the World Wide Web on copyright law has, of
   course, been enormous. For recent, reliable discussions of the issues,
   see Sanford G. Thatcher, 'Fair Use: A Double-Edged Sword,' *Journal
   of Scholarly Publishing* 32, no. 1 (Oct. 2000): 3–8; and Robert Spoo, with
   a reply by Harold Orlans, edited and introduced by Michael Cornett,
   'Current Copyright Law and Fair Use: The Council of Editors of
   Learned Journals, Keynote Address, MLA Convention 2000,' *Journal
   of Scholarly Publishing* 33, no. 3 (April 2002): 125–47.
4 The style manuals dominant in specific fields are well known to students and faculty in those fields; less familiar, perhaps, are the specific instructions to authors posted on their websites by publishers,
   journals, and academic and scientific societies. Authors hoping to
   be published by a given publisher or society should make the effort
   to locate the latest version of such instructions by searching the
   Web. In some instances, downloadable word-processing templates
   and instructions for electronic submission are also available for
   authors from publishers' and journals' websites.
5 Advice about avoiding sexism and racism abounds, to the point of
   confusion about terminology that really is acceptable. Style manuals
   often have useful discussions of political correctness, and two books
   are recommended: F.W. Frank and P.A. Treichler, *Language, Gender,
   and Professional Writing: Theoretical Approaches and Guidelines for Non-
   sexist Usage* (New York: Modern Language Association of America,
   1989); and M. Schwartz and the Task Force on Bias-Free Language of
   the Association of American University Presses, *Guidelines for Bias-
   Free Writing* (Bloomington: Indiana University Press, 1995).
6 The most helpful and succinct handbook on the uses of graphs is that
   by Shirley M. Peterson, *Editing Science Graphs*, which is no. 2 in the
   Guidelines series (ISBN 0-914340-14-X) published by the Council of
   Science Editors (formerly, the Council of Biology Editors). For ordering information, see http://www.councilscienceeditors.org. Despite
   its title, this guideline is useful to authors as well as editors and dis-
   cusses graphic forms used in other fields besides the sciences.

chapter seven

Basic Advice for Novice Authors

ALLAN H. PASCO

Authors should learn something about the business of publishing. Such knowledge will help them find appropriate outlets for their work, understand what services various presses offer, and prepare to fulfil their own responsibilities in these days of increasing automation and rising costs. Manuscripts dealing with topics of broad appeal may attract one of the high-volume trade publishers, though most academic books are written for professors and graduate students and therefore have narrower audiences. University presses are committed to serious scholarship, though they can no longer ignore sales potential and have had to close their doors to books so specialized that they will interest only a small circle of scholars. Books on the more rarefied topics should be produced by short-run publishers whose work often appears under the imprint of a monograph series. Such focused series are almost invariably run by people in the thick of the field who may even be highly regarded experts. These presses frequently do the best job of publishing and marketing work for a limited audience.

Authors' desires for public exposure of their work must conform to the realities of publishing. The first step is to give clear-headed consideration to the strengths of various publishers and to the personal benefits authors wish to receive from their books. I recently read a manuscript with broad topical appeal, for example, which should have been published by a high-profile trade publisher, but the author felt that without an agent she could ill afford a potentially long-drawn-out process of finding a prestigious publishing house. She chose instead to settle for a small press that requires subventions but that promised both a rapid decision and expeditious publication. By opting for speed and the familiar over the unknown, she gave up both the possibility of high-volume sales and the anguish of knowing that her manuscript would probably end up on a slush desk, where 'over the transom' submissions generally land at the big, better-known houses. Such trade-offs may be possible and are to be considered.

Generally, there is more prestige in publishing with a well-known trade house. If one believes one's work has potential for wide readership, and if one has the time and patience necessary to secure a niche in the hotly competitive commercial market, this avenue should be attempted. A good university press may, however, be the wiser choice, since its editors know the academic market and are used to dealing with professors. It is usually more prestigious to publish with a university press than with a monograph series. Still, as said before, monograph series specializing in a particular field may be more appropriate because of editors' special skills and contacts. Because small press editors are usually active themselves in the area of their publications, they should know how and where to address their offerings. They may also give more personal attention to authors and to their works. Perhaps more important, while monograph series will usually keep books in print and available for decades, trade publishers and, less frequently perhaps, university presses remainder unsold books within a few years after the initial high-volume sales cease. Authors have to balance relevant considerations of this nature.

Obviously, writers want to have their work in print as soon as possible and at no financial cost to themselves. They may have thought the matter through no further than that, but other needs are just as real and often just as pressing. Professors are responsible for communicating the knowledge they discover. Of course, they teach what they learn to their students, but they should also share with their colleagues across the field. In order to do so, it is vitally important that their books be reviewed, listed in appropriate bibliographies and catalogues, and displayed at appropriate conferences. Effectively targeted mailers are essential. A well-placed space ad or two might also be helpful, though David Lee Rubin, publisher of Rookwood Press, reminds me that while ads may increase the press's prestige and do wonders for an author's ego, they seldom sell enough books to justify the expense. By no means least important in the hierarchy of authorial desires, publishing scholars deserve to have their effort rewarded suitably – whether with monetary payment, promotion to a higher rank, or professional recognition. Authors must be concerned about each one of these factors and should learn what benefits different kinds of publishers offer. It may be necessary to accept some less-than-ideal situations in order to secure the press the author deems most desirable. Few beginning authors can find a publisher willing or able to meet all their goals.

Once a writer feels convinced that the manuscript is not only accurate, complete, honest, useful, and professionally formatted but also well written,[1] major decisions remain. A list of presses that might be interested in the manuscript and that could expertly produce and market the book should be compiled. Careful evaluation of the publishers' missions can save time. Should one pursue publication with a trade, university, monograph, or even electronic press? Though the latter is probably not yet sufficiently well established for most academics,[2] the others need to be considered. A major trade publisher will probably not be drawn to a study of ladybugs' flight paths or Baudelaire's father, while subjects of this kind may be just the thing for a particular monograph series. The astute author can glean some information about publishers through research on the press's website and in the library. Publishers' catalogues are revealing. Does a press's list of publications include similar or related books? Publishers often welcome the opportunity to market several offerings together, for they would appeal to the same buyers and thus spread advertising expenses. When a press has an extensive list in a certain area, specialist buyers seek out its offerings.

I have been approached repeatedly since the publication of the first version of this essay by mostly – but not always – young authors who complain, 'My book is not being reviewed. What can I do?' The matter is important. I know of a volume published in Germany which should have been widely used but was not because the press did little to announce its availability. I learned of it only several years after publication in a subsequent article by the author. In another case, a publisher let a book go out of print before the reviews were all out. And, to tell one final horror story, the first book of a former colleague, who is now one of the top people in his field, was reviewed only once, a state of affairs that caused his promotion to full professor to be held up for years. It was a good book, but the series in which he published was known as a dissertation mill and not highly esteemed. As a result, journals that regularly review related books apparently decided not to bother with it. Furthermore, the publisher distributed very few copies of the book for review. Marketing directors know that only one in ten volumes sent to appropriate journals will elicit a review. Nonetheless, as I have learned from inquiries, few academic presses send out more than fifteen or twenty copies. Purdue University Monographs in Romance Languages (PUMRL), the series I formerly edited, distributed between thirty and forty. An effective press will solicit the author's help in deciding which journals to include in the mailing, and some editors (and authors) regularly call on the goodwill of their journal editor friends and acquaintances in asking that reviews be arranged.

While it is an open question as to whether book reviews sell many books, professional reviews are vital to an author's career. They will be taken seriously in considerations for raises, promotions, and other positions. Authors should find out whether or not a series succeeds in having its books listed in the major bibliographies and reviewed in the appropriate journals. Choose a book or two in your field that was published two to four years ago by the press you are considering, and then check several of the most important reviewing organs that normally review such works. Was the book reviewed? If not, beware! Ask the press (or journal) whether they send out (or receive) review copies. It may be simply that your colleagues are being slow in reading and reporting on offerings. It may, however, be that the press only 'distributes announcements' or only 'sends review copies on request.' Few review editors will request anything but the most obviously important books. They seldom bother for unknown authors or for presses with less than sterling reputations. Sometimes, the mistake of going to a press with a poor review record may be overcome by making a special appeal to journal and review editors or by encouraging a well-known colleague or two to wear your colours. It remains, however, best to avoid presses with a poor reviewing record, though such a press may be preferable to discarding your work, especially if you have respect for some of its other offerings.

Does the press or series advertise in suitable journals? Do its books appear at conference exhibits? More important, does it regularly send out direct-mail advertisements? If authors or their advisers do not receive mailers from a particular series at least once a year, I would hesitate to submit manuscripts to it. Increasingly, publishers are also turning to Internet listservs. Both experienced and novice authors want their books in the hands of scholars, a happy pass that will occur only if potential buyers know about the new publication. While many libraries have standing orders with some presses and series, standing orders are never enough to assure a wide reading audience. Direct-mail publicity and book exhibits are essential to the effective marketing of academic books.

Authors concerned about the reputation of their books should never send manuscripts to a vanity press. These publishers seldom request jurying, for they care more about the amount of the subvention than about the manuscript's quality. Even though vanity presses may receive and publish a good manuscript now and then, the questionable reputation of the press taints all of its publications, which all too often die a quick and silent death.

Presses should have manuscripts externally evaluated or 'juried' by specialists who know the field and can reasonably be expected to judge the quality of the work accurately. Such readers frequently make worthwhile suggestions to improve the manuscript. Although some presses often have to request support from the author or author's home institution to cover expenses, they are different from vanity presses in that they rigorously evaluate manuscripts, generally accepting somewhere between one in five and one in ten submissions. Former professors and other professional acquaintances are often a fount of useful information about names and reputations that should be considered when deciding where to send a manuscript.

Ask other authors, mentors, colleagues, and friends whether or not a specific publisher is prompt in evaluating work. Three months to reach a decision for or against publication of a book manuscript is desirable; six is not unreasonable. But when the delay stretches beyond that, there should be an explanation. It is acceptable for an author to query a press about a manuscript three to four months after its submission has been acknowledged. The editor's response will give the author an indication of when a further query would be in order. Reputable presses will acknowledge receipt of a manuscript and respond to queries. On two occasions, I have had presses take eighteen months to make a decision on a book of mine. Even if the editors have difficulty with over-committed, ill, or thoughtless readers, six months should suffice for an editor to issue a contract or return the manuscript. Several years ago, I received a letter from a friend telling me that the editor of a university press had promised him a decision by the end of the week on the manuscript he had submitted three months earlier. Either my colleague or the editor was confused, because several days later I received a letter from that editor asking me to evaluate the manuscript. I rather suspect that the submission had been allowed to get lost on a desk. Well-connected professors in the field will know which presses take an unreasonable amount of time to reach a decision for or against publication.

Once authors have established and ranked the lists of presses that satisfy their requirements, they should write to ask whether or not the publishers would be interested in considering the manuscript. It is perfectly ethical to query five or six at a time (though in North America actual submissions should be limited to one press at a time unless permission for multiple submissions has been granted). The letter of inquiry should be on an institutional letterhead, if the author has the right to use one, and the text should be relatively short, to the point, and engaging. A page or a page and a half should suffice to give the writer's credentials and a brief synopsis of the offering. Include a two-or three-page summary or outline of the book and a brief curriculum vitae that stresses publications and major professional successes (leave off courses taught, papers offered, and reviews written, unless there is a pressing reason to include them). It is vital that this material be extremely well written, since it may be the author's only chance of securing an editor's attention.[3] Some people send a sample chapter or two, but do not send the entire manuscript. If the return of the materials is desirable, postage should be enclosed (I usually fasten it to the letter with a paper-clip). For European presses, one may send a cheque, money order, or international coupons, though given the high cost of postage, rather than paying for its return, it may be best to suggest discarding the submitted copy in the case of requests for changes or rejection. A self-addressed, stamped envelope (SASE) should always be included, even when the return of the manuscript is not requested. Editors appreciate the courtesy. Authors should ask the press to give some indication of the length of time between acceptance and publication. No more than a twelve-month delay is possible, though such prompt action requires everyone's cooperation. More than two years is excessive. Beginning authors of very specialized work should probably not expect royalties. At the novice stage, it is far more important that the book be published and read by appropriate people. Such initial success will pay off royally in the long run.

When a press answers a query favourably, it is important to respond professionally.[4] Answer any questions. Submit only a neat, legible manuscript. Careless proofreading usually leads to quick rejection. Today, a clear photocopy is acceptable, though the press may request assurance that the author is not submitting another copy elsewhere. If two copies are expected, send two. If the publisher wants your text on disk, comply with the request.

Ideally, the editor has carefully considered the earlier query and has invited the author to send the entire manuscript only after being assured that it corresponds, on the surface at least, to the press's needs. In the best of all possible worlds, after inviting submission of the entire manuscript, the editor quickly verifies its appropriateness to the press's future needs. A manuscript's unsuitability for a planned publishing direction may bring a quick rejection, though it has little or nothing to do with the merit of the manuscript. Again, ideally, the acquisitions editor will send out the manuscript for external evaluation only after such basic decisions have been made. Specialist readers should by training and orientation be capable of giving a manuscript a competent reading, though that does not always happen. The evaluator may have a bad day, may be over-impressed by minor problems early on in the manuscript (as was Gide when he rejected Proust's manuscript of *Du côté de chez Swann*), may in fact be an ignoramus or so committed to a particular approach that even-handed evaluation is impossible. If everything goes well, the manuscript will be sent out for a second reading, perhaps a third, before making its way to the editorial board for the final decision. Of course, not all submissions are accepted. At any point in these proceedings, things may go awry. Although one of my manuscripts received two very positive evaluations at one university press, for instance, it was turned down without explanation when it reached the editorial board. I still do not know why. The next press that considered the manuscript accepted it, and the book was well reviewed. Later, it was reprinted twice, before being reissued in a second edition.

Changes are almost always requested, more or less emphatically, before manuscripts are accepted, and authors should consider such suggestions with humility. Prima donnas seldom write great scholarly books. Still, editors sometimes require changes that cannot be made without distorting the work. Authors then have no choice but to argue their case (which I have seldom done, though I know those who have appealed successfully) or withdraw the manuscript and try another publisher. When the manuscript is turned down, presses will usually send along copies of the anonymous evaluations – occasionally one must ask for them – which the author may study at leisure. The ability to learn from rejection, the courage to persist in the quest for a publisher, to try again (repeatedly, if necessary), marks the successful professional. Persistence pays. One of the most surprising and helpful experiences of my life came one evening early in my career when two well-published professors of international reputation began in my hearing to compare the ways editors had turned down their work. Several of the stories were amusing, but most were not. Some of the rejections were decidedly vicious. It may help to recall that every author has had work refused and has felt professionally and personally rejected, sometimes often. The only people who do not receive rejection letters or slips are those who do not submit their writings.

Should everything go well and the book be accepted, the author's work is not done. He or she is expected to submit a manuscript that is neat and that demonstrates serious consideration of the evaluators' suggestions (with a letter explaining briefly what has or has not been done). After the revisions are approved, the best presses send the manuscript to a copy editor, who will note spelling mistakes, typos, grammatical errors, and infelicities, and ask many questions having to do with clarity. While the author and editor may have differences of opinion, a polite note will generally clear them up. Certainly, every author I have known has learned much from the copy editor.

Authors should be willing to help sell their books. It is false economy to save money by sending author's copies only to mother. Buy enough additional copies, at whatever discount the press offers, to ensure that the book will reach the readers who will be most important to its reputation, though only the press should send review copies to journals. Promotional material provided by the publisher should be distributed suitably. Friends want to know about the book, as do experts in the field. The idea, of course, is to spread the word as far as possible in the target audience. Often it leads to more reviews, citations, and quotations, all of which can enhance sales of the work. With the author's help, a book stands a better chance of reaching the appropriate audience, who, one hopes, will be impressed.

During the entire process, it helps if the author understands something of the difficulties confronting publishers. Most presses are struggling against the current to provide a much-needed service. Those monograph series specializing in literary studies confront particular difficulties. It is a tough business, in which no one is getting rich, and dedication and self-sacrifice are the rule. Editors and editorial boards often work for nothing but the hope that they are accomplishing something worth-while. If specialist readers are paid anything to evaluate authors' work, it is usually a ludicrously low sum, pennies per hour of effort. Though the academic book market is well seg-mented – technical vocabulary meaning that marketers know who buys publications – it is very thin; that is, the potential readers and their libraries are spread across the world, with sel-dom more than a few buyers in one place. Professors do not purchase great numbers of books, and libraries have to make hard purchase choices with their limited funds. As a result, sales are sparse. What is worse, the profits are often low or non-existent. Academic publishing is a high-risk enterprise, indeed.

Anyone with even rudimentary knowledge of business knows that there are only three standard cures for low or non-existent profits: the press must decrease costs, or widen the margin between cost and selling price, or increase the volume of sales. In general, the low sales of scholarly books about specialized topics like literature decree limited print runs of from two to seven hun-dred copies. Unfortunately, as the number of books published in the run goes down, the unit cost per volume rises, increasing the expenses that must be recouped from each volume sold.

Although the obvious solution to low sales is to sell more books, no one is quite sure how to exploit the academic market more successfully. If published space advertisements seldom justify the expense, direct-mail advertising is sensitive to increases in mailing costs and has limited results (response rates often average 1 or 2 per cent). Every increase in the price of postage decreases its cost-effectiveness. Few publishers hope to make dramatic improvements in the sales of books on such things as literary criticism, especially at present, when the exciting new critical schools of a few years ago have become passé and hold little interest. Price – at least if within limits – does not seem to be the decisive factor in sales. Still, prices cannot be raised outrageously. A number of my colleagues, for example, have not even asked their libraries to order a certain Swiss publisher's reprints because of the staggering prices. Certainly, scholars seldom if ever buy such expensive volumes themselves. On the other hand, low prices do not seem to stimulate buying significantly. One monograph series went broke a few years ago despite very reasonable prices.

What, then, does a publisher do? If cutting the price does not increase sales volume, if raising the price eventually meets sales resistance, and if no one seems to have any strikingly effective ways to find buyers, one can cut costs. Here again, given that publishers have seldom been profligate and never been profligate for long, there are limited avenues for cost reduction. The expenses of paper, bindings, and other physical features can be reduced only so much. People who like books like good-quality books. I, for example, have long tried to avoid asking my students to buy the lower-quality paperbacks, because it infuriates me to see the books in tatters after a second reading. We expect high-quality bindings, acid-free paper, and if not hard at least durable covers, so that even soft-cover books will have a long, useful life in our hands and on our shelves. Publishers can and often do keep prices within reason by soliciting several bids internationally for printing, storage, and distribution, but that too takes time, and, as we all know, time is limited and has its own costs.

Monograph series have certain advantages over university and trade publishers when it comes to keeping costs within limits. They are usually small operations with dedicated helpers who donate lots of free time. Books are often stored, not in expensive warehouses, but under beds. Many monograph series have reduced costs by cutting editing to the bone. Reviewers who flog publishers for clumsy style and typos are behind the times, since these days the author is more commonly responsible for such matters. As publishers increasingly insist that authors present their manuscripts either as photo-ready copy or in machine-readable form, [5] authors become even more directly related to their finished books. Although the university presses that published my most recent books, for example, used copy editors, I was asked in two instances to enter the changes onto a disk myself. The results of decreased editing and professional typesetting are often regrettable: annoying misspellings, grammatical errors, or stylistic infelicities; too much or too little leading (interlinear space); infrequent or incorrect hyphenation; running heads that are either unattractive, uninformative, or absent. Printers and typesetters once took care of widows and orphans and of rivers of disruptive white space as a matter of course. Today, because of automation, such problems often need to be corrected by authors and editors. While all presses hope costs are being cut in ways that will not affect quality, they are successful only to the degree that, when necessary, scholars are sufficiently well trained or motivated to be their own copy editors.

The only other solutions to these problems that I have discovered involve increasing the publisher's capitalization. Occasionally, the press may secure additional internal money either from a host institution or from the editor's family or second job. One publisher told me glumly about a colleague who, having won a lottery, was asked whether he was going to retire and live the good life. He responded, 'No, I think I'll just keep on publishing until it's all gone.' Trade publishers once took profits from best-sellers to subsidize an occasional 'public service' volume of poetry or criticism. In the current economic climate, marked by corporations syphoning funds during reorganizations and leveraged buy-outs, such philanthropic activity has become almost non-existent. A few major university presses rely on their own golden eggs to generate operating funds. One thinks of Oxford's Scofield Bible, an edition of the King James Version first published in 1909 and still widely used, or Chicago's *Manual of Style*. But most university presses, though they have gone on bended knee to the great sugar daddy in the administration building, get little additional support, and even risk losing what they have, since universities are themselves under financial pressure and have been known to take the short-sighted view that publishing represents a non-essential function. In fact, successful publishing ventures are an important indication of an outstanding university.

That leaves external funding, and we arrive at subsidy publishing. University presses and monograph series are increasingly looking to agencies like the Humanities and Social Sciences Federation of Canada or the U.S. National Endowment for the Humanities, to authors' home institutions, or to the authors themselves to meet the heavy costs of short-run publishing. Most often, the press expects the subvention to meet the production costs, today between $3,000 and $6,000 for the normal two-hundred-page book. Some subventions are less.

Book publication is a difficult business that requires struggling more or less well to keep the many needs in balance. The issue is not 'to publish or not to publish?' Nor is it even 'to publish or perish.' The issue is how to publish in such a way that the author and the field benefit for many years to come. Then everyone is happy – printer, publisher, editor, and author. That seldom happens, however, unless everyone knows what to expect and works together for successful publication.

NOTES

I am very grateful for the advice of Professors John S. Brushwood, Alain-Philippe Durand, David Lee Rubin, and Robert E. Ziegler.

1 For detailed guidance, see Walter S. Achtert and Joseph Gibaldi, *MLA Handbook for Writers of Research Papers*, 5th ed. (New York: Modern Language Association, 1999) and *The Chicago Manual of Style*, 14th ed. (Chicago: University of Chicago Press, 1993). *The Elements of Style* (New York: Macmillan, 1959), by William Strunk, Jr, and E.B. White, is a masterpiece of helpful guidance and has been frequently reprinted. Joseph M. Williams's *Style: Toward Clarity and Grace* (Chicago: University of Chicago Press, 1990) lays out a sensible set of principles for revising one's prose, as does Francis-Noël Thomas and Mark Turner's elegant *Clear and Simple As the Truth: Writing Classic Prose* (Princeton: Princeton University Press, 1994). H.W. Fowler's *A Dictionary of Modern English Usage*, revised by Ernest Gowers (New York and Oxford: Oxford University Press, 1965), though passé in some respects, is considered the standard of academic writing and remains a witty, useful guide.

2 Electronic publishing continues to be the subject of much controversy. For a positive view, see John Unsworth, 'Electronic Scholarship; or, Scholarly Publishing and the Public,' *Journal of Scholarly Publishing* 28, no. 1 (Oct. 1996): 3–12. For a negative view, see Sven Birkerts, *The Gutenberg Elegies: The Fate of Reading in an Electronic Age* (Boston: Faber and Faber, 1994).

3 William Germano's guidance on finding and approaching presses is excellent, with many a useful insight for preparing the manuscript for publication; see *Getting It Published* (Chicago: University of Chicago Press, 2001), 43–96. Good advice on these and other aspects of publishing is also to be found in Alida Allison, Terri Frongia et al., *The Grad Student's Guide to Getting Published* (New York: Prentice Hall, 1992), 153–85; Ralph E. Matkin and T.F. Riggar, *Persist and Publish: Helpful Hints for Academic Writing and Publishing* (Boulder: University Press of Colorado, 1991), 94–108; and Mary Frank Fox, *Scholarly Writing and Publishing: Issues, Problems, and Solutions* (Boulder: Westview Press, 1985), 33–98. J. Appelbaum and N. Evans, *How to Get Happily Published* (New York: Harper & Row, 1978) remains a helpful, encouraging overview.

4 Useful suggestions may be found in Trumbull Rogers, 'Make My Day: A Reasonable Request,' *Scholarly Publishing* 22, no. 1 (Oct. 1990): 40–4.

5 For an excellent introduction to preparing camera-ready copy, see Helen R. Tibbo, 'Specifications for Camera-Ready Copy: Helping Authors Be More Productive,' *Scholarly Publishing* 25, no. 4 (July 1994): 221–32. Daniel Eisenberg's 'In-House Typesetting on a Tight Budget,' *Scholarly Publishing* 21, no. 4 (July 1990), especially 214–16, is very useful, though Macintosh users of Pagemaker or Microsoft Word will find the author's prejudice in favour of the IBM-compatible MS-DOS machines and the preference for WordPerfect surprising if not ill considered.

Index